Texas Girl

Texas Girl

a memoir by

Robin Silbergleid

DEMETER PRESS, BRADFORD, ONTARIO

Demeter Press logo based on the sculpture "Demeter" by Maria-Luise Bodirsky <www.keramik-atelier.bodirsky.de>

Printed and Bound in Canada

Front cover artwork/design: Chris Corneal

Library and Archives Canada Cataloguing in Publication

Silbergleid, Robin, author
      Texas girl / Robin Silbergleid.

ISBN 978-1-927335-38-3 (pbk.)

Cataloguing data available through Library and Archives Canada.

Demeter Press
140 Holland Street West
P. O. Box 13022
Bradford, ON L3Z 2Y5
Tel: (905) 775-9089
Email: info@demeterpress.org
Website: www.demeterpress.org

for my children

Part I

1.

MY DAUGHTER WAS CONCEIVED over the phone during a conversation with my on-again, off-again something-or-other. At this moment, we were mostly off-again, given that he was living four states away. Still, he'd call me at odd hours, harass me about my early bedtime and short stature and leave me wondering why I had spent the better part of graduate school fawning over him and buying overpriced lingerie from Victoria's Secret. There was something about his honeyed voice, coaxing me into doing all sorts of things I shouldn't do, from the very first time we didn't go out on a date.

The last time I'd seen him I was sitting at my desk, in the corner of the kitchen where a table was supposed to go, pecking out the sentences of my dissertation on my laptop. The desk sat under the window that faced the outside corridor of the apartments, like a cheap motel, and his face peered at me through the glass, long fingers held over his eyes like a visor. I felt like I'd been caught doing something incredibly private, putting one word after another in a slow seduction of language, Coltrane crooning on the stereo. I wondered what he saw when he looked at me, chewing my thumbnail, bare legs folded beneath me on the chair as I wrote. Did he see a woman he loved, or a painting by Modigliani, hands and breasts and mouth?

I hadn't seen him in more than a month, since the day he'd packed his books and copies of *Esquire* magazine in liquor boxes and headed to Texas to start a new job. He hadn't told me he was coming. I opened the door and buried my face in his T-shirt. We stood in the doorway a long time, not speaking. It was so quiet I could hear a talk show from my neighbor's living room. He smelled tender, like talcum powder and laundry fresh from the dryer. He pulled me wordlessly to the bedroom where he peeled off my clothes like the skin of a precious fruit and took me to a place beyond metaphor.

We did not conceive a child that night, but a single-celled idea implanted itself in the wall of my uterus and then slipped out, painlessly, like an early miscarriage, a few weeks later. As I listened to the sound of his voice thrumming through cross-country phone lines, I remembered the weight of his body on top of mine, and I imagined a holding a daughter who had his long toes and my eyes. Sometimes, like tonight, in the autumn air crisp with possibility, she was all I could think about. The force of my desire surprised even me.

I sat in my ratty terrycloth robe on the oversized armchair in the corner of my room while the cats chased each other back and forth across the length of the apartment. The last time he was here I sat on his lap, my head in the eloquent curve between neck and shoulder, while he read poems from the books on my shelves, his voice warming me in places starved for touch. I missed him. I missed his late night visits and roaming hands and the heat of his breath in my ear. I wanted to be with him, in his lumpy bed in a city loft, doped up on the sound of his voice, not alone in a student apartment with plastic covers instead of real storm windows to keep the chills at bay.

I wondered where I would be living in a year, if I'd be stuck in the same town in a state of prolonged adolescence, all of my twenties given up to the great writers of the twentieth century; if I would spend my weekends, as I did now, shuttling between the public library and the apartment, checking out books about babies and home decor and hiding them under the bed like a teenager's stash of porn. At my feet lay page after page of job descriptions, professorships in creative writing, American fiction, women's studies. I imagined myself in a huge lecture hall, prattling on about the conflict between work and family that still faced women today and Sylvia Plath's choice to take her own life at the ripe old age of thirty, and then coming home and eating tuna fish, giving the cats the juice from the bottom of the can, and watching TV until colors fizzled into migraine. Something in the vicinity of my uterus cramped.

"Did you see the one for Grinnell?" he asked. "That looks perfect for you."

"Yeah."

"You don't sound particularly enthusiastic." He was doing that thing I hated, playing pop psychologist, echoing back what he heard me say.

"I just want to have a baby," I think is what I said.

"You're twenty-seven." He said it in a way that it could have meant anything. You're twenty-seven, so wait. You're twenty-seven, so of course you want to have a baby. He was good at giving those sorts of indefinitely interpretable answers. I called him Dr. Boy to my friends.

"No, what I mean is, I don't think I want to do this job thing." What I didn't tell him was that my dearest friend from grad school had just sent me a chipper email telling me she was expecting a baby in April. I looked up her due date on a website that gave information about each week of pregnancy; this week, it said that women who are experiencing nausea might find relief in eating high protein snacks before bed.

"Well, you can't exactly be a stay-at-home mom if you're not married."

I'm not sure what I wanted him to say, but that wasn't it. I didn't want to be married. And I certainly didn't want to be a stay-at-home mom, with a brood of toddlers tugging my knees and dumping grape juice all over the carpet. He kept talking, and as he talked there was a flash of clarity, bright and honest as orgasm. Something in me shivered and burst open, something beyond narrative, beyond the predictable life story of man plus woman equals baby, and in the words that traveled across the phone lines, something marvelous began to take shape. When I got off the phone, I flushed my birth control pills down the toilet. This time next year, I could be somebody's mother.

2.

EVERY DAY DESIRE GREW. Two cells became four became eight. First, she was a pea-shaped blur, and then the body elongated, the shape of the head separated from the shape of the body, then limb buds and genitals; from embryo to fetus, she gained ounce after ounce, inch by inch, every day becoming more herself. I dreamed her into existence. I followed her growth in the books I checked out from the library, *What to Expect When You're Expecting* and *A Girlfriend's Guide to Pregnancy*. I did what women trying to get pregnant are supposed to do. I stopped taking any drug that might cause a birth defect. I ate something green every day. I took prenatal vitamins and calcium supplements. I took long walks, breathing in the smell of old grass and fallen leaves. I went to bed early, resting a belly full of promise on the pillow, and rose to the sounds of children playing in the churchyard beneath my window. Desire swelled in me; I rested my hand on the soft spot beneath my navel and breathed.

3.

IN DECEMBER, I took her with me to my grandmother's funeral, an idea tucked in the pocket of an ovary. The child never left me. I turned the thought of becoming a mother over in my mind and rubbed it like the worry stone I held for most of my sophomore year as I tried to stay calm and focused in class.

This is what I knew: the soul of a Jewish person does not rest until she has a child named after her. In this belief my mother held absolute certainty. It was a lesson as deeply engrained as the fairy tales we read each night before bed. I was given the Hebrew name Rachel, after my great grandmother who had shared a bedroom with my mother when she was a girl. I had only seen Rose in black-and-white pictures where she wore full-length skirts and button-up boots like on *Little House on the Prairie,* her dark hair pulled taut in a bun. She looked stern, like a schoolteacher who slapped the hands of her ill-behaved students with a ruler. That didn't bother me. I understood that I was a living tribute to someone who had died, and that I would not have my proper name, if not for those years my mother spent listening to her bubbe breathe in their shared room on Cypress Avenue, her old woman's perfume thick in the air, and her black-soled shoes lined up at the foot of the bed.

So I had always known that I would not name my first child for anyone other than my own grandmother. Her memory was ripe as marrow in my bones. I wrote poems about her collection of demitasse I imagined to be my private inheritance. I conjured her from family stories, how she and Aunt Mary used to play on the roof of their family home, dressing and undressing their dolls. I was the eldest of her five grandchildren; it only made sense that my child would bear her name. It hadn't really occurred to me until now that my grandmother would need to die in order for this to happen. Jewish law demanded it.

When my period started at the cemetery, the cramps hit me hard.

We stood beside the plain pine coffin chanting the Mourner's Kaddish for my grandmother, shivering in our wool coats. Grief was heavy in our mouths, like the moans of a laboring woman. Weeks ago, at the hospice center, the nurse had said that death is a process like birth is a process. I turned the analogy around in my mind, until my grandmother became the infant who took her last breath as all of us became the mother's body struggling. I wanted to scream. Nausea rose up from an acidic pit of loss in my stomach. I wouldn't throw up. Not now. I tried hard to keep myself still, arms crossed at my waist, gloved hands digging into my ribs. The ground was winter slick and hard beneath our feet. I slowed my breath and watched the long exhale turn to smoke from the cold. I held my mother by one arm and my sister held her by the other, and as we started walking back toward the black limo, she folded into herself, a tight fist of pure sound. Blood pooled between my thighs. At last, my grandmother was delivered.

We coiled around each other, my mother, my brother, my sister and me, in the limo that carried us back to my grandparents' home. I remember my head in my mother's lap or her head in my lap, our bodies merged as they had been before my untimely birth, and as we wept I told her, "If I have a girl, I will name her after Grandma." It was the closest I'd come to telling my mother that I wanted to have a child. Oh, in some way I had been dreaming of her for years, a little girl in navy blue shoes and a red dress, new for the high holy days like the dresses Grandma Anne had bought for me year after year to go with my school shoes from Buster Brown. Now, since the last time I'd seen Dr. Boy in September, since my twenty-eighth birthday a few weeks ago, since Grandma's long dying, the baby had become more than a doodle in a sketch book or an early draft of a poem. I felt her like a solid mass in my uterus. And I wish, oh, how I wish, that I'd been able to tell Grandma about the baby in those long months she was dying, in those long months I dreamed her up.

I do not know how much of my life my grandparents under-stood—my choice at twenty-one to go to graduate school to study literature, my choice to be poet, professor— but they were my biggest champions, the slim volumes where my writing appeared lined up on the bookcases in their guest bedroom, testament to money well spent, decades of their work poured into possibility as my grandfather wrote checks to pay for my first year of graduate study, the only one of my eleven years of higher education not covered by tuition waiver or fellowship. I had thanked them. But I wanted to pay them back in a lan-guage they would understand, a good job, a great grandchild. And I was on the cusp of both.

Just weeks ago, in the midst of my grandmother's dying, I had gotten a phone call about a job. This was Dr. Boy's doing, of course. If nothing else, he was rational about it. I couldn't have a baby unless I had a job. So I went to Staples, bought a package of 9 x 12 envelopes and a ream of crisp white paper, and spent hours tinkering with the sentences of my cover letter and the placement of punctuation on my curriculum vitae. I took fifty-some envelopes to the post office and sent them scat-tered cross-country, and then tried to forget, dreaming my days away with the baby in my ovary, until one day the phone rang.

It was eleven or so in the morning, and I rarely answered the phone during the day—I had a rule about those sorts of things, it was always a telemarketer or a relative I didn't want to talk to—but I remembered I was applying for jobs and, sure enough, it was a kind-voiced man from A College Far Away saying they wanted to interview me at the national convention in a few weeks. I did what we were supposed to do. I asked him to hold on for a moment while I ran around looking for my planner, tripping over the library books scattered on the floor, so I could write down the important details. I asked him who would be conducting the interview. I asked him if there were any supplementary materials I could send him ahead of time. I thanked him sincerely. And when I hung up, I danced to Madonna's version of "American Pie," which I will forever associate with getting good news. Then I remembered my grandmother was dying. I stopped dancing, put my hand on the place I imagined my uterus to be, and sat down on the floor. Something I couldn't name washed over me in waves of nausea and grief.

It was the beginning of December, and snow was falling in Indiana. The cats sat on the back of the couch and watched my neighbors come and go in the parking lot. An egg left my ovary and worried itself down the fallopian tube, a child not yet created and already dying. I got up and scratched the tops of the cats' heads in that crest between skull and ear. They purred contentedly. I picked up Dannon, the smaller cat, because she liked to be held like a baby, and let her rest her head on my shoulder. I walked her around, bouncing the way I'd seen new mothers do to soothe colicky infants. My heart slowed until I couldn't hear it pounding in my ears anymore. My next-door neighbor slammed her door. I startled. I didn't want to end up an old woman with sixty-five cats and wire-rimmed glasses. I set Dannon down by the food bowl. It was time to be practical.

In the office corner of the kitchen, I sat cross-legged in the beat-up desk chair and looked at the website for A College Far Away, Nowhere, North Texas. The posted job description said they wanted a specialist in American literature, 1963-present. And to be sure, my own personal narrative of

American literature revolved around the year that Sylvia Plath had published *The Bell Jar* and then killed herself, her two small children asleep in the next room and a manuscript of new poems neatly arranged on her desk. Not that I planned on saying that during the interview. As I contemplated the words on the ad, I wondered how I had not seen so clearly weeks ago that this was a perfect job for me. I could have a job and a baby. I looked at the sprawling map of Texas and started imagining a child I might have with Dr. Boy next year. I spun out elaborate fantasies where we lived in the city that was half-way between each of our jobs, occupied both halves of a duplex so we could have rooms of our own but just pop in next door for complicated ethnic meals and hours on the couch with a movie, passing the baby between us. It would be like leaving the adjoining door open in a hotel.

"You want company?" I could almost hear him say, leaning against the door frame while I held the baby high on my shoulder, with a cloth diaper under her face to sop up the drool.

"Sure," I would say, handing her over to him. He rubbed his nose in her dark brown curls and kissed the top of her head. She looked so small, hardly bigger than his hands. He took her and sat down in a rocking chair, singing to her softly while I watched, rolling the kinks from my neck. It was cozy as a scene from a Pottery Barn catalog. I sighed.

I knew I was getting ahead of myself; I hadn't even told Dr. Boy about the job yet. But there were pictures of these people I started imagining as future colleagues, pictures with German shepherds and tiger-striped cats and smiling grandchildren, with overstuffed bookcases and desks piled with papers and cups of pens, and I thought they seemed like such wonderful people already that maybe it wouldn't matter that it was Texas. Already I was homesick.

A few days later, what was left of the family gathered in the hospital, my mom and aunt and uncle, my cousins, my sister and brother. What was left of my grandmother lay in the hospital bed, her body shriveled to bones. Even her head looked smaller, thin tufts of hair unwashed and unstyled. Until this fall, when she had taken sick, she had gone to the beauty parlor every week to have her hair done, a pre-Sabbath ritual. I remembered when I was very small, she wrapped the hair right by her ears in pink foam rollers lined with a single sheet of toilet paper, to keep the curls during the week. Once, she wore a housedress and floppy pink slippers with rubber soles. Once, when I was six and she first got sick, she wore a wig of curly dark hair. It snagged on the branch of a tree as we walked home from the park. The branch reached down like a hand and plucked it off her eggshell head and it hung there, waiting for her to reclaim it. How she laughed. How we all laughed, telling and retelling that story. Now her throaty laughter was gone but there was a quiet peace in the leave-taking of her body. The muscles of her face slackened in sleep, the skin of her cheeks sagged toward the pillow.

I had never seen a dying person before.

My grandfather had called us on Thanksgiving, and I am not sure exactly what he said to my mother, but the next day she was on a plane to New Jersey, just as she had done when I was in first grade and something in grandma's abdomen burst, infection spreading everywhere in the dark cave of her belly. "We got problems," I think is what he said. The doctor said she might have had a stroke. She never really woke up, not more than to mumble a few words in a watery dream voice. The diagnosis didn't really matter. She was tired. When I visited that last time, the only thing she said to me, with her eyes clamped shut, was "did you eat on the plane?" The grandmother I loved was already gone. We fed her spoonfuls of pudding from the hospital cafeteria and said our goodbyes.

I wanted to tell her that as soon as I could manage it she was going to be a great grandmother. I thought if I could tell her anything to make her get well that would be it. I wanted to whisper it in her ear.

I still don't know what stopped me. I gave her another spoon-ful of tapioca and smoothed her cotton blanket. Still, I'd like to think that behind her tired eyes, she knew.

At the cemetery, we gathered and prayed around the unmarked grave. And I thought, this not-quite-child I carry in my body, she was there before my own birth, in the eggs that rested inside me as I grew inside my mother who had grown inside her mother who now rested in the ground. She was born dying and she would be born again in her namesake. I promised. And my grandmother, who had once played with her dolls on the roof of a farmhouse, now lay as naked as she had come in to this world, sighed, giving up her breath to the future.

4

"I'M THINKING ABOUT HAVING A BABY," I said and passed Aimee the plate of *naan*. We were having dinner at an Indian restaurant a few blocks from the hotel where our interviews would take place, the scent of curry powder thick in the air. Since the last time I'd seen her, when we'd sat in a coffee shop in her neighborhood and she'd spoken longingly of walking a son or daughter to the elementary school close to their house, she'd cut her hair, which had once fallen to her waist in mahogany spirals, and conceived a child. What I didn't say, back then, back when I was just a friend visiting from out of town was *I want one, too.* All day, when I wasn't pacing back and forth in my hotel room, making up answers to imaginary questions and fretting about my interview with A College Far Away, I thought about how I would tell Aimee about The Baby Plan. It was a plan I revealed to my friends one at a time, soliciting advice, making it real. Aimee was the only person I knew who was actually on the way to becoming a mother. I told myself that shouldn't matter, but her opinion seemed to count the most.

"Wow." She put the plate down and swallowed hard. Her whole body seemed to contract. Her eyes narrowed as she took it in. I thought of UFOs spinning through the night sky on Sunday night TV, as we sat on the twin bed she'd covered and turned into a couch and ate pizza laced with garlic and feta cheese.

What I didn't tell her was that Dr. Boy and I might have

conceived a child when he visited just before I left for the convention.

"Where did that come from?" Aimee asked, rubbing a spot just under her breasts, where I imagined her baby's feet would be. She was about five months along, and if she sat hunched over, which she planned to do during her interview, it was almost impossible to tell she was pregnant. Now she sat more upright than I remembered her ever doing, letting the kid stretch out.

"Honestly, I don't know." I watched my fork push some rice around my plate. My cheeks felt flushed in a way I usually associated with embarrassment. "When I hit twenty-seven it was like a small bomb went off in my uterus. And now, with my grandma dying...I don't know, Aime, it's just one of those things I need to do. I just don't know how."

"Well," she chuckled, "I see half a dozen good looking hows just walking around in here." She smiled wistfully. "But it in a way, it was the same with me, I'd look at pregnant women and tell Rich, I want that *now*. Scared the crap out of him. Took us six months to conceive, so by then he was pretty much used to the idea."

I smiled back. I felt something between us shift and settle, like the aftermath of a storm. I remapped the cartography of our relationship. Since she married Rich and moved away, I couldn't even bring myself call her on the phone. Sometimes I thought I hardly recognized her. Back when we lived in the same place, we piled into her small car to buy groceries and return books to the library. Back then we went to the gym at seven in the morning and graded papers in coffee shops in the evenings. We ate Chinese dumplings and talked about boys, we shared performances of the Indigo Girls and campus productions of *The Vagina Monologues*. It was like being married to the woman who lived upstairs, she'd once said. Now she seemed like she lived in another galaxy, Hetero World. I felt like I was encroaching on her time when I sent her an email. Dr. Boy said that's how it was with married people, but I don't think he really understood.

When Aimee married Rich, I felt like a jilted lover. Now, our conversations were as stilted as a date with an ex.

"Hey, did I tell you I'm having a boy?!" She beamed from ear to ear.

"No. Oh, boy. Wow. Are you happy about that?" I couldn't quite picture her having a son. She hated the puffed up masculinity of team sports.

"Well, when they did the sonogram, the doctor started showing me the parts. This is a leg and this is a leg and, oh, that's not a leg, and I think I must have said, *a penis? What am I going to do with one of those?* But, yeah, it's exciting. Rich is really excited, which is good, because I'm going to make him change all the diapers. I'm growing a penis. Really." She snorted. "Hold on a sec? I've got to pee."

I watched her get up from the table and smooth down her shirt, the long gray knit top she'd bought during a shopping spree one Friday night when we decided, collectively, to take the night off. She walked to the bathroom in the back corner of the restaurant, her hand rubbing circles in the small of her back. Someone was in the restroom, and while she waited just outside the door, I saw her look back at me with soft eyes. I tried to imagine her in the doctor's office, holding Rich's hand as the doctor moved the sonogram wand across the globe of her abdomen. I knew, with absolute certainty, that was a moment I would never share. And I thought, if I could have everything I wanted, it would be Aimee and her baby in the downstairs apartment and me and my baby in the upstairs apartment and we would take the babies to mommy and baby yoga classes and sit in library story hours together and take turns mashing organic sweet potatoes and bananas to feed our children. It would be like she never left. Where Rich and Dr. Boy were in this fantasy I couldn't quite figure out. A kid commune, I think Aimee had once said. She seemed happy, blissed out on estrogen. I wanted that.

I thought, just maybe. Dr. Boy and I hadn't talked about the baby plan in any concrete way, but when he'd shown up in my apartment last week, ostensibly to help me get ready for my interview with A College Far Away, the tutorial took place in my bed, without a condom, much less my new black suit. We'd never had sex without birth control before. And as he moved inside me, I thought about how beautiful our child would be, with *café au lait* skin and dark chocolate eyes. Afterward, I held my legs in the air while he went to the bathroom to wash up. How I'd missed him.

I missed the way he would show up at my apartment at all hours of the night and lie down with me in a bed that was much too small for two. Those nights of endless possibility, he was a poet, writing elaborate metaphors for all the things that he was going to do to me. I missed his voice, wrapped around words like *bourbon*, like *breast,* right next to my ear.

Loneliness unfurled in me like a fern in spring. Aimee had moved away and Dr. Boy had moved away and our other friends were all getting jobs and getting married and having kids. And there I was, alone, waiting.

That night before the convention, when Dr. Boy came out of the bathroom, he put his boxers back on and sat on the edge of my twin bed, rubbing my belly like a cat's. My cervix cramped, and colors sizzled and sparked by my right eye. He said something knowing, like holding your legs like that is good for conception. I hadn't told him I'd gone off the pill, but there's a part of me that has always wondered if we were both trying to get pregnant, not like Aimee and Rich who'd bought ovulation test kits from CVS, but by simple acts of omission and chance. If we had a child, we would be bound together for life. I didn't know if that was a good thing.

I didn't know what it meant that before I met Aimee for dinner I saw two half moons of red on my underwear.

5.

ALL WINTER a life was taking shape. A life bigger than my three rooms, than quiet nights spent on a Goodwill couch, a lone mattress on the floor. A life tucked in a pocket of my abdomen, a life of mother and child I imagined growing cell by cell. All winter as I walked from here to there, tracing the path down Indiana Avenue in my wool coat, I thought about warm afternoons at the park. I dreamed the days, the small girl and I getting out of the station wagon and walking hand-in-hand on the gravel path that led to the playground. She raced ahead to the swings and I followed her, watching her auburn curls ruffle in the wind. "Mommy, come!" she called. I helped her climb into the tire swing and spun her, this girl half my height, head thrown back in toddler ecstasy. "More big spin, Mom, big spin again!" and I spun her and both of us were dizzy with a life that never stood still, gulping down summer air.

She climbed on the monkey bars, step by step, rung by rung. At the top was a plastic bubble that resembled a space ship. I stood outside and she pressed her monkey face against the glass and giggled and giggled. She hung from the roof, singing at the top of her lungs "mommy called the doctor, said no more monkeys jumping on the bed!" My Hannah, my monkey girl, my dead grandmother's great-granddaughter. I dreamed her into existence. She was as real to me as myself and I couldn't imagine living without her.

A few weeks after the convention, I sat in the auditorium listening to a visiting poet read, my mouth full of day old garlic noodles. The taste wouldn't go away. I brushed my teeth, and it was still there like a bad dream. The man sitting next to me smelled like patchouli, and I wanted to retch. I thought, here it is, here in the taste of my mouth, the smell of this room, is early pregnancy, the baby a secret in the curve of my uterus, growing cell by glorious cell.

My period was late. Or I thought it was late. It hadn't settled in to any sort of normal rhythm since I'd stopped taking the pill. I bled a little bit at the interview, crescents of red spotting my new underwear, not really enough to call it a period, and nothing else since. The book I'd been combing for advice, *Taking Charge of Your Fertility,* said that sometimes women bleed when an embryo implants in the wall of the uterus. I willed her to stick.

I couldn't concentrate. As the poet read, words flapped around my face, unreadable as wings. At home the pages of my dissertation lay on the floor like puzzle pieces that wouldn't quite fit. I taught my classes. I went to my tutoring job. And through it all, the image of this curly-haired girl floated in the corner of my eye until she grew into a migraine. I vomited and slept and the next day it would all start over again.

I counted the days since I'd seen Dr. Boy and thought if somehow we'd managed to conceive, I would be about six weeks along. I was ravenous. I craved eggs and bacon, French toast in a pool of maple syrup. I went to the local deli and ate. I was sure the waiter could see the desire for a child in my eyes, that the colleague I ran into with his wife would nod knowingly at my abdomen, cloaked in a long flannel shirt. Finally, I went to the drug store. I didn't know what brand to buy, didn't know how to properly pee on a stick. The name Clear Blue seemed prophetic, so I paid and took it home, along with a package of prenatal vitamins and calcium supplements. I read the directions, I peed, I waited, and after ten minutes no second line appeared.

I was too shocked to cry. The next day I started bleeding for real, and by the time I went to Texas for the second interview, things had stopped tasting funny. Still, there was a rumble in my empty belly, hungry for the child who didn't grow.

I bought pink lingerie to wear under my suit for the campus interview. Dr. Boy lived only an hour away and we talked about him driving up to see me after I gave my presentation. It was Valentine's Day, and the small part of me that believed in fate thought the timing couldn't have been more perfect. The one glitch in my plan was the setting. The college had put me up in a bed-and-breakfast across the street from campus, overwhelmed with Texas-sized furniture and more floral wallpaper than I'd ever seen. The old couple who owned the place was inescapable, as the front door opened into their living room, where they sat watching TV. It was on last night when I'd arrived, and it was already on this morning when I walked downstairs for breakfast. I could hear it as I shoved some eggs around my plate and sipped coffee so black it soured my stomach. It would never work to bring a boy back to my room.

"Where did you grow up, honey?" The old woman, whose name might have been Mrs. Hart, set a plate full of heart-shaped waffles on the dining room table.

"Chicago. The suburbs, anyway." To anyone who lived there, the distinction was critical.

"This is a long way from home." She smiled. Texans, I'd noticed, smiled an awful lot. "So what made you want this job?"

"Well," I swallowed my coffee and turned a response over in my mind like a snow globe. I didn't know much. But I sensed that all of this—the B&B chit chat, the car drives between here and there, the private meetings in faculty offices—was part of the interview. How would I fit in the department, the college, the town? "I've always really liked the idea of working at a small college, and there's a lot of opportunities here to teach great students the things I'm interested in." I smiled. "And the school has a great reputation."

"That it does." She wiped her hands on her floral print apron and picked up a green dish full of overcooked eggs. "You want some more eggs, sweetie?"

"No, thank you." I couldn't stop thinking about that white blob in the swirl of the yolk, the part I always pulled out carefully with a fork and washed down the drain before I scrambled an egg. Someone told me once it was a miscarried chick. I cleared my throat. "I think I'd better head across the street. But thank you. Breakfast was lovely."

I walked through the living room littered with knick-knacks and back issues of *Reader's Digest*. Mr. Bed and Breakfast snoozed in the Lazy Boy recliner, while on the TV some nameless talk show host gave advice to teenagers who'd dropped out of school when they got pregnant. The girls chewed gum and bounced their babies on their laps. I sighed. Everywhere I looked I saw children and pregnant women. I grabbed my backpack, shrugged on my coat, and made my way across the street to meet with the Dean.

In the dim light of February morning, the campus was small, and my first reaction was to think it was ugly. Almost all the buildings were a mustard-colored brick, and it was possible to walk leisurely from one end to the other in less than ten minutes. The college library, when I walked through the stacks on my tour, was the size of the public library in my hometown. Set between the Administration building and some two-story dormitories, the quad was flat and gray and quiet, crisscrossed with sidewalks painted by sororities. It was cold, but it wasn't real winter; the students I saw hurrying to their first class wore sweatpants and sandals with socks. As sun came out, nameless professors wearing bright sweaters traversed the concrete paths, making their way to the student union to fill up travel mugs with coffee or iced tea. Except for the ten minutes between classes, there were hardly any students outside; I imagined them holed up in their dorm rooms writing papers due later that day or chatting with friends in other faraway places on their cell phones. All day, when I wasn't smiling and nodding politely in conversations with senior faculty, I wrote in my journal and left Dr. Boy more messages than I could count.

Every time I went to the bathroom, I put on more deodorant and reapplied my lipstick. I didn't recognize myself in the mirror. I looked bloated and worn out.

That evening, after my presentation, I had dinner with a group of students in the cafeteria. We sat at one long table in a small room adjacent to the main dining hall, listening to the sounds of conversation about classes and off-campus parties balloon around us. The students I sat with were smart and beautiful, and they'd given up their Friday afternoon to listen to me talk and share a meal with someone who might, or might not, be their professor in the fall. I didn't know what I was supposed to do to get them to like me, but I knew that their liking me was vital to getting the job. We ate spaghetti and salad, and some of the girls had soft serve ice cream cones or chocolate chip cookies for dessert. They told me, in hushed tones, that the cookies had been rationed because so many people used to steal them for midnight snacks. Between bites, they asked questions. I almost spat out my Coke when a bright-eyed blonde asked, "Do you have religious, uh, aspirations?"

I swallowed and smiled. I had been tipped off by a faculty member that some of the questions might be inappropriately personal. "Well, I grew up Jewish, but for me that's more of a cultural thing than a religion."

The blonde girl smiled back and took a sip of her Diet Coke, and the girl sitting next to her asked me what kind of music I liked. What they wanted, it seemed, was a friend, or a big sister who gave them advice and occasionally let them borrow her clothes. "Well, right now I'm into what a friend of mine calls 'chicks with guitars.' Folksy stuff, Dar Williams, Paula Cole."

"I love Dar Williams! Didn't she just come out with another album?"

"I'm not sure." I couldn't even remember the title of the CD that I'd popped into my laptop that morning. I imagined her going back to her dorm room and filling out the questionnaire about how well she'd liked me as a prospective faculty member and writing something like, "She knows absolutely nothing about pop music, but I guess that's okay."

Eventually one of them asked me about how I conducted my classes, whether I liked to lecture or have big discussions, if I used papers or tests or both. And as I answered, I imagined them sitting in a circle in an air-conditioned room, taking diligent notes during winding conversations about poetry and gender discrimination and the great women writers of the twentieth century. It was an image as romantic as a scene from a movie, like *Dead Poets Society*, only for girls. I pictured myself stacking up my books as the girls lingered after class and then walking across the tree-lined campus where even now, in February, the grass was relatively green, going up the stairs to a corner office filled with books and stacks of paper to grade, sitting down with a large cup of coffee and reading, Beth Orton crooning on the stereo. It was an English professor's dream, to be sure. But where, in all of this, was the baby?

I conjured her at seven months, swinging back and forth in one of those battery-operated swings, lined up next to other babies swinging back and forth, in a dim room at a commercial daycare center on the main road in town. She sucked on a pink pacifier while she swung. A skinny blonde girl, who couldn't have been older than nineteen, grabbed a crying baby from a swing and laid him on a changing table in the corner of the room. She pulled off his dirty diaper and put on a clean one, and then she put him back in the swing and started all over again with another crying baby. There were eight of them in total.

The baby that was my baby didn't look happy to be there. I

wasn't sure what that meant, but it didn't seem like a good omen.

I was deeply ambivalent about the job. I wanted it desperately. I wanted to sit with those girls and talk about poetry, I wanted them to come to my office and ask for help writing papers, and when that was done, share a cup of tea and gab about the TV shows they liked and the other classes they were taking. And I wasn't sure that wanting the job was a good thing.

Everyone I met on faculty was delightful, to be sure. As we drove from here to there or chatted in their offices and over meals, we talked about our favorite books and our students. They talked about their families, how long ago they'd finished their studies and packed up their children's clothes and toys and came to the College and never left. They traveled to Japan and Patagonia and all sorts of far away places and then they came home, to their dogs and cats, their kids and spouses. Some of my imagined future colleagues were grandparents already, pictures of chubby-cheeked babies on the corkboards next to their office doors. They were good people. And here I was, not even finished with school yet, imagining being one of them thirty years down the road, and regretting giving up my life for the Texas flag.

There is no other way to say this: I panicked.

I watched Texas take shape in the car window as one of my prospective colleagues—a soft-spoken man with glasses and a tweed jacket, a wonderful breathing stereotype—gave me a tour of the area. He drove me past the hospital, where he said a helicopter could ferry patients off to the nearest big city; he drove me down the long farm road full of signs boasting about new subdivisions, sprawling ranch homes set high and lonely on a hill; he drove me through the ramshackle town, where there had once been race riots, and now buildings were boarded up and run down, just a lone family owned restaurant with its bright blue door lighting up the square. He drove me past the bookstore, which mostly rented videos and sold used CDs, and the public library that was small enough to be a single family home. As he drove and talked, I realized I hadn't met a single faculty member who was under the age of forty.

I saw the huge Texas flag waving from pick-up trucks. I saw big hats and cowboy boots. I felt myself getting smaller, sliding down in the passenger seat. I didn't know if I could live in the Middle of Nowhere, North Texas.

When I got back to my room that night, I put on my pink pajamas and left Dr. Boy another message. He was out, I supposed, at the bar, drinking bourbon or maybe smoking a joint. He'd come home and see the blinking light on his answering machine and maybe he'd think of me, naked in a room less than hour away, and maybe he'd think about the last time we'd had sex, with my legs up in the air. And maybe he'd wish that I wouldn't get the job, that, only an hour away, was a little too close for his comfort. When finally we talked, later that night, his voice was more like barbeque sauce than honey.

The next morning, when the department chair dropped me off at the airport, he said I reminded him of himself all those years ago. I said I hoped that was a good thing.

As I boarded the plane, I was hit with a sorrow so fierce it almost knocked me down. I settled into my seat, with my black notebook on the pull-down tray. The flight attendant wheeled the drink cart up and down the aisle, asking, "can I get you something to drink, hon?" She had big bouffant hair and wore hot pink lipstick. Even the thought of moving to Texas was turning me into a xenophobe. I wrote a little, putting down the pros and cons of the job. I pictured my not-quite daughter swinging on that swing. I pictured taking her home to an apartment on the outskirts of town, putting her in a high chair and feeding her mashed up peas from a little glass jar. I pictured her wearing a cowboy hat and shooting a toy gun at our cat. I cried.

From the window of the plane, the checkerboard of Indiana farms had never looked more beautiful.

6.

IN A HOSPITAL several states away my best friend was giving birth to a son. I didn't know this for a fact—it's not like she called me to say she had gone into labor—but it was almost a week past her due date and all day I had been cramping in what I decided had to be sympathy pains. If it could happen to expectant fathers, why couldn't it happen to psychically in-tune best friends?

It hurt. It started as a niggling feeling in my abdomen, the prodrome of menstruation. And it spread, wrapping around the small of my back and down to the tops of my thighs. I moved from my bed to the bathroom to the bed again, lying down in the fetal position or squatting on the toilet. I was shivering, sweat beading my forehead and chest. I thought about women I'd seen giving birth on television. I held my arms across my abdomen and groaned.

I imagined Aimee flat in a hospital bed, feet in stirrups, a doctor in a green mask standing between her legs saying, "push, that's it, push." She squeezed her husband's hand and bore down, their son's body half in half out of this world, his shoulders caught on her pubis bone. The baby's heart slowed until the monitor shrieked. The doctor snapped, "Let's go, Mom. He's out in one push or we need to do a C-section." Then he thrust the metal forceps inside her and pulled while she pushed, a nurse pressing the top of her uterus and Aimee screaming as her skin stretched and tore.

In the bathroom of my apartment, I screamed along with

her, only I wasn't giving birth to a child but fistfuls of blood. I felt them move deep in my womb and inch down with each cramp. I pushed with the pain. When they finally emerged, the clots were meaty and dark. They looked like liver. They looked like what I imagined bits of placenta to look like. I held them in my hands and let them go. One by one I flushed them down the drain.

I sat in the tub while it filled with water as hot as I could stand. I closed my eyes and listened. I could hear my heart over the sound of the rushing water. When the contractions started again, I opened my eyes and watched the water around me blossom into red flowers, like the tulips that were budding across campus. In a few days, they would wilt and droop, their petals raw and swollen as bruised mouths.

I don't know how many times I emptied the tub and filled it again. I broke the blackberry curdles and smeared them on my abdomen like paint. And then I slept.

When Aimee called a week later to tell me they were home from the hospital and okay—the baby was sick with an infection for a while but they were okay—I propped the phone on my pillow while I shivered in bed. I told her how happy I was, and I went into the bathroom to change my pad. The garbage can overflowed with plastic wrappers and sanitary napkins wrapped in toilet paper. The floor was stained with the child I wouldn't have.

I thought about the night I'd conceived her, dreamed her into being as Dr. Boy's voice swam through the phone line like some kind of metaphorical sperm. I thought about the last night we'd spent together, now almost four months ago, with his hand resting on the flat plane of my abdomen. I thought about the negative pregnancy test I'd tossed into the Sunday morning trash. None of it made sense.

There is no other way to say this: the bathroom looked like a painting by Frida Kahlo. When I finally saw the ob/gyn, she gave me the diagnosis of 626.2— excessive or frequent menstruation—flat, inadequate syllables. What happened to me was no metaphor. Now, years later, words are all I have: nine months of want given up like a late miscarriage. What does it sound like to you?

7.

I KNEW IF I EVER HAD a nervous breakdown it would begin in the supermarket. Standing in the aisle that implausibly housed feminine hygiene products, pregnancy tests, and a whole host of baby supplies, including Pampers Swaddlers, manual breast pumps, and jar after jar of Gerber's baby food, I resisted the urge to throw a temper tantrum. Barely. I needed tampons. Lots and lots of tampons. And right in front of the tampons stood a woman with a belly so gravid that she clearly did not need tampons. Or a box of Clear Blue Easy. But she'd set up shop there, fussing with a container of Cheerios that her son, who looked to be no older than nine or ten months, cheerily let fall from his chubby hands. I remembered the monologue I'd done in college, from Christopher Durang's play *Laughing Wild*, in which the narrator threw an absolute fit about cans of tuna. Sometimes I wondered what would happen if I just broke down, like the character in the play, and started screaming in the middle of the feminine protection aisle. Or sent the president of the grocery store chain a note on university stationery explaining why it was just plain cruel to put the boxes of Kotex next to the boxes of Huggies.

I pulled my watch out of the front pocket of my backpack. I was supposed to meet my friend Lee in the packaged food section. Lately, she had a thing for the California rolls they sold in plastic packages at the shi-shi grocery store that had just opened in town. It was supposed to be in and out, back to my apartment for dinner and a video.

There was no way around the pregnant woman. I pretended like I was looking at merchandise, comparing prices for a long time. I looked at my watch again. "Excuse me," I finally said.

The woman handed the baby a Cheerio before she looked up. "Oh, did you need to get in here?" Her eyes gradually came into focus, like she'd just swum up to the top of a pool after being submerged for a long time.

My pulse thrummed in my ears. I smiled. If it worked in Texas, maybe it would work in an Indiana supermarket. She pushed her squeaky cart to the other side of the aisle, to the pacifiers and plastic spoons, bumping her belly against the display of baby bottles. The whole aisle seemed to sway along with her. I steadied myself. I grabbed two boxes of Tampax, tossed them into my shopping basket, and bolted.

I found Lee in the frozen foods section, deliberating between Eli's cheesecake and Dove Ice Cream Bars. "Hey," she said, "there you are. Did I tell you about the day I ran into Professor Johnson when I was buying frozen fishsticks?"

"No," I said. "Get the cheesecake."

She put the Dove Bars back in the freezer. "It was horrible. I mean there I was, wearing that flannel shirt I always wear when I write papers—I was supposed to be writing a paper for his class!—and my hair was in this ratty bun thing and I was wearing my glasses. Frozen fishsticks! Who buys frozen fishsticks?!"

"Why does it matter that you were buying frozen fishsticks?"

"It's just so White Trash!" Lee had a love-hate relationship with her Indiana roots. On good days, she called herself The Voice of Rural America. Her best poems were secondhand anecdotes about family members from towns so small they celebrated new stoplights; her portraits were generous and forgiving. "What took you so long, anyway?"

"I forgot something. Come with me?" Lee followed me back to the baby aisle, and the pregnant woman was still there, hunched over, picking up Cheerios as her son wailed.

I pulled a three pack of ovulation test kits from the shelf and put it on top of the cheesecake.

"Good grief," Lee said, rolling her eyes. "Let's get out of here."

There were babies everywhere, smartly dressed celebrity babies on the covers of magazines and fat drooling babies in shopping carts in the checkout line.

"You know," Lee said, "I was reading this article about parthenogenesis. At some point it might be possible to have a baby without using sperm at all. Even that sheep Dolly was cloned from only eggs. Cool, huh?" She put the sushi and cheesecake on the conveyor belt and stuck her tongue out at the toddler in front of us. He giggled.

I wasn't sure what Lee really thought of The Baby Plan, but she watched the parenting magazines pile up on my coffee table and she listened to the grocery store meltdown anecdotes without passing judgment.

She was my new Aimee, I sometimes thought. Since her boyfriend had finished his degree and returned to Russia, we spent virtually every free minute together. We worked together at the Writing Center, coaching foreign exchange students on the intricacies of English grammar. We shared our writing. We went to poetry readings and movies. She showed up on my doorstep at 10:00 at night with Popsicles in a cooler that looked like it was used for organ transplants. She moored me.

"My purse still smells like chicken," she said, absently, pulling out a ten-dollar bill from her wallet.

"I'm sorry, really, Lee-Lee. I'll buy you a new one." The last time we had dinner I convinced her to put my leftover Moroccan chicken in her handbag, and the sauce leaked all over. It was her favorite one, with a print of a Japanese woman on the side. It reminded me of a childhood nightmare.

"I'm sure Freud would say you did it on purpose, R.P. Get me something I can use in California, okay? Something goofy, you know, like my monkey lamp."

"Sure thing. When I see a Monkey Lamp Purse at the store

I'll pick it up." I swiped my credit card and tossed the receipt into the plastic bag with the OPKs. "Let's get out of here?"

"You know you're going to have a baby with Dr. Boy," she said as we walked toward the car. "I mean, how can you get a job in Texas and not have a baby with Dr. Boy? It's fate. It's the only way the story can end."

"Glad to hear you're putting that narrative theory class to good use." I looked at her with soft eyes. Her caramel-colored hair was twisted in a red plastic doohickey that looked like a crab. She wore impossibly short shorts and a long white peasant blouse. She was the kind of smart, leggy girl that Dr. Boy would go for, I thought. "Should we pick up a movie at the library? Your turn to pick."

I sat in the stadium in my rented cap and gown beside my dissertation director who had made a special trip for the occasion. It was ghastly hot for May. Beneath the black gown, my red silk dress soaked up beads of sweat. Around us, thousands of nameless undergrads, some of whom had been my students or whose papers I had tutored, were tucked into the bleachers like we were attending a ball game. I looked around and tried to see my family. Lee was somewhere, in her own rented cap and gown, receiving her diploma cover. We'd meet up later for dinner, before her parents came to take her home for the summer. Beside me, Judith was saying something about why we call graduations commencements, about the relationships between endings and beginnings. I was on the cusp between here and there, finished with one thing and moving on to the next, both at the same time. The journey to Texas stretched ahead of me like a well-traveled cliché.

By the time the college actually offered me the job, winter had turned to spring, and I'd decided that moving to Texas was a good thing. My new colleagues sent me long, winding notes welcoming me to the department, suggesting places to live and inviting me to their homes when I came back to campus to visit. The girls I'd met over dinner sent me emails asking for the reading lists for my fall courses, for copies of my poems, for advice about going to graduate school. I felt wanted.

The Ph.D. candidates lined up and took our place in front of the bleachers, the President of the university calling off our names one at a time, and on the side, a photographer took pictures of us in our mortarboards that were all too big or too small, my own pinned with black hairpins and still dangling precariously from my head. I knelt in front of Judith so she could place my doctoral hood over my head, and in the photograph that my mother took we are small shapes in a swarm of people bending and bowing as if in prayer. Over the hum of voices, I thought I could hear my grandfather call my name. He'd helped pay for school. I went to the ceremony only for him.

Those last weeks, I let spring ripen in me, like the daffodils and the red and yellow tulips opening up all over campus. I couldn't sit still. I walked from my apartment to the library and back again, as the Bradford pear trees snowed white petals. I drove across town to the co-op to fetch apricots and blood oranges. I drank green tea in the bookstore café and read copies of *Martha Stewart Baby* and *Hip Mama*. I ripped out pictures of cribs and changing tables from catalogs. I started taking my basal body temperature with a pink thermometer and recorded it every morning on sheets of graph paper. I made lists and I planned.

Lee helped me box up my stuff and choose a moving company. The last time I saw her we watched movies in my living room and drank melon liqueur.

"Maybe I can stop in Texas on the way to L.A." she said.

"Maybe."

"You're going to be a mom, R.P."

"And you're going to find some beautiful man to marry." My drink tasted like a Jolly Rancher candy. It soured my mouth. I emptied it into the sink and watched her drive away, a box of my books in the backseat. Somehow, I knew I'd never see her again.

I walked around campus saying my goodbyes. I took pictures with a disposable camera. I made mental notes of the places I loved. The gates that separated campus from town. The statue of a young couple. The old well house. The bench near the steps that led to the library, the spot I thought of as my own secret garden. The large globe on the first floor of the building that housed the English department, which was my first memory of the place. I took pictures of my office, bare except for stacks of old magazines and a calendar with a pig on the cover. I took pictures of the boxes stacked up inside my apartment, filled with books and years worth of notes, wool sweaters I wouldn't need in Texas, and tank tops and shorts that I would.

This was the place that had shaped me, the place where I had grown into myself, where I formed habits that I imagined would last a lifetime. Yoga classes and long weekend walks; a predilection for gourmet coffee and peach tea; notebooks with ladybugs or Monet prints on the covers; Uniball black pens Aimee and I bought by the box from Staples. Everything I had ever known was here, within four hours driving distance of Chicago. My best friend was married and had just given birth to a son. My other friends were going their separate ways, to new graduate schools and new jobs. My grandmother was dead. And I could officially call myself professor. The daughter I'd been dreaming of all these months, I would become her mother in Texas.

8.

I SHOULD HAVE KNOWN how the visit would go when Dr. Boy picked me up at the airport.

The whole plane ride I had scribbled lists in my notebook: lists of things I wanted to buy for the new apartment, lists of books I wanted to read, lists of baby names, lists of things I wanted to accomplish at my new job, lists of reasons to have a baby now and lists of reasons to wait. I felt alive, hormones thrumming my cells. Maybe Lee was right; maybe having a baby with Dr. Boy was inevitable.

But the night before, I'd had a dream that Dr. Boy was living with another woman. She hauled a big red suitcase from her car's trunk and left it on his front porch; he lugged it in, grunting a little as he pulled it over the threshold, while I waited in the next room. They kissed in the entryway to the kitchen, a place that looked suspiciously like his old apartment in Indiana, and then he said, "I'd like you to meet my friend Robin."

We were not a couple in any proper sense of the term. We'd started not-dating the year we worked together as teaching assistants for a large lecture course. He called me almost daily, under the pretense of talking about the class, and then he invited me over to his place and we talked and ended up in his bed. Those first few weeks, I got caught up in the thrill of desire and domesticity. I cooked him dinner, extra spicy Thai curry or beef braised in Guinness. He assembled bookcases in my living room, a basketball game on in the background. Sometimes, we'd watch movies I'd never watch on my own, like *Austin Powers,* and sometimes we'd watch *The X-Files,* which I'd always done with Aimee. Sometimes we even went out. One of the first nights we spent together, he said to me we'd have to be careful, and even under the circumstances, it became clear he wasn't talking about birth control. What he didn't want was to fall in love. I should have told him to get dressed and go home. But his touch was addictive. And he was smart. We'd spar about this or that and then he would pull off my clothes, seducing me with Mary Oliver and Karl Marx. He gave me a reason to buy silk nightgowns and shave my legs.

I could have loved him. And for a little while, I think I did. But it's hard to let yourself fall in love with someone when they make it clear that the last thing they want is to fall in love with you. We were together and not together, and I wondered which other women in our graduate program he had slept with. I was always falling for men who were involved with other women, men who were afraid of committing. A friend had said to me once if she didn't like sex with men she would be a lesbian, and that seemed to me exactly right.

So when he left for Texas, which was in one of our "on again" times, we agreed we could get involved with other people, and we also agreed, or at least I remember agreeing, that we would tell each other if it ever became an issue. I decided that the dream was prophetic.

When I got off the plane, I expected him to be waiting for me. This wasn't something that we had talked about; it was just how my family and everybody else I had ever visited had done things. It honestly never occurred to me to ask him, or tell him, where to wait. He wasn't at the gate. He wasn't at the baggage claim. And when I'd fetched my luggage and waited for fifteen minutes I began to panic, not sure whether I should be angry at him or worried that he'd gotten into an accident somewhere on the highway. I checked my watch again. Finally, I went up to someone in a uniform who worked in the lost luggage area and had him paged.

I leaned against a pole, watching a lone suitcase go round and round the luggage carousel. Everyone else had claimed their bags and hugged their loved ones. I bought a bottle of water from a vending machine. I watched taxis come and go out the window. When a new batch of bags stared turning the carousel, he finally appeared, gesticulating wildly and ranting about traffic and parking spaces. He ushered me out into the beastly Texas heat, and there we were, a couple that wasn't quite a couple, me visiting so I could find an apartment close to my new job and wondering what me moving to Texas meant to him anyway. It was the sort of thing most academic couples dreamed of, two tenure-track jobs with an easy commute, but like I said, we weren't a couple in any ordinary sense of the word.

That night he took me to dinner at a local café, a place I gathered he spent most of his nights with a drink in his hand, talking with the owner and the other regulars who came to be his friends. They were in bands. They were undergraduates with part-time jobs who'd taken one of his classes. They were beautiful women with dark hair and Texas tanned skin.

One of them came over to our table to chat. She hovered so close that if he turned his head he had no choice but to stare at her breasts. I watched him watch her.

"This is Robin," he cleared his throat. "She just got a job at the College."

"Oh, that's great," she said, and I could tell she was trying to figure out what that meant to him.

She invited him to some party later that evening, and before she walked away, he put his hand on her forearm. Nothing particularly erotic but I saw in his dark eyes the pull of her body, and the space between us seemed to widen. It was a gaping chasm that threatened to swallow me up.

I moved the salt and pepper shakers, the little bottles of ketchup and mustard, to give myself something to do. I didn't really want to look at him. I didn't know what I was doing, moving to Texas. What else was there for me in that huge state, but the job and him?

"She hangs out at the coffee shop where I work sometimes," he said after she'd crossed the room. "We talk about music and movies. Good to not have the professor hat on sometimes, you know?" His voice was soft, almost apologetic.

We stayed at the table for a while, sharing key lime pie off a white plate, talking about my new job, and then we moved to the bar where some of his friends were sipping from bottles of Shiner Bock and laughing. I wanted to be back in his apartment, just hanging out and listening to Chet Baker, his hands exploring the curves of my back. One of them invited us to his place for a drink. I said something to tell Dr. Boy I needed to leave: it's been a long day, or I have a headache, or I need to call my mom.

As we walked back to his car, he said, "I'm not really ready to call it a night. You mind if I go out for a little while?"

The sun was just beginning to set, and I felt chilled from the air-conditioned café. "No." What else could I say? He pulled me into his chest and held me, his hand on the back of my neck.

"It's good to see you, Robin."

"Yeah," I said, pulling away from him, "I've missed having you around." But he didn't seem any closer, standing beside me, than he had when he was four states away.

All I remember of the drive home is Fiona Apple crooning on the car stereo.

"There's clean sheets on the bed," he said, when we got back to his place.

"And juice in the fridge if you want anything. I'll be back in a couple hours."

I lay in his bed for a long time, rolling from side to side. I watched the red numbers on the clock change. I got up and drank a glass of water and scribbled in my notebook. I lay down in the bed again, but it was big and empty, and I kept rolling into the well of his long body in the mattress. Finally, I took the comforter and spread it out on the floor like a preschool mat. When he came home, he slept on the futon in his office.

I sat at the Starbucks halfway between Dr. Boy's place and my new job, writing in my notebook, trying to make sense of things. I'd assumed that when I moved to Texas things would be like they used to be, with him showing up at my apartment at all hours of the night, and us going out occasionally for dinner and a movie or even a party with his colleagues. But now, thinking about the bar and all those leggy Texas women in his circle of friends, I wasn't so sure. I wondered which of the pretty girls he was sleeping with. I wondered if he was ever going to tell me. I wondered if I would ever ask him.

At the next table, a woman sipped iced tea and rocked an infant seat with her sandaled foot. Her hair was pulled back in a chic ponytail at the nape of her neck, but there was a white smudge of spit-up by the collar of her black shirt. Her eyes were glazed over, I assumed, from hormones and lack of sleep. When the baby fussed, she reached down and popped the pacifier, dangling from a plastic clip, back in his mouth. Then she stroked the blonde fuzz on top of his head.

"How old?" I asked, when she looked up.

"Four weeks."

He was the same age as Aimee's son. "He looks so peaceful."

"Yeah, he really likes being out of the house. You have any kids?"

"No," I shook my head. "Not yet."

I sipped my coffee. I tapped my pen on my notebook. I chewed my thumbnail. I looked at the mother and her new baby. I thought like I thought about my dissertation or a poem, turning the ideas around until they settled and came into focus, clear and bright as a Polaroid.

I'd been going about this all wrong.

I had always wanted a child. When we played dress up as children, my friends were princesses and brides, donning their mothers' old negligees and slipping their feet into oversized golden shoes and saying their vows, while I stuffed a pillow into my mother's maternity clothes and pretended to be pregnant, my prince nowhere to be found. In the pictures of my mother's album, I stand in profile, displaying my belly like any proud mama-to-be. Maybe the answers were there, in those childhood games.

I thought, if I have a child with Dr. Boy, it would be exactly like it was with my father, going to visit him on weekends when he would take my sister and me to movies and restaurants but never really talk to us; he'd drink his black coffee and read his newspaper and ask the same perfunctory questions about grades on tests and extracurricular activities every week, never remembering the answers. Or we'd play *Star Wars* action figures with our stepbrother while our father sat in the Lazy Boy and watched ball games and reruns of *Star Trek* on TV until he'd gotten the eight hours he'd paid for with his child support check, and then brought us home. Oh, I have no doubt he cared about me but he wasn't really part of my life in any positive way. In the end, I'm not sure he knew how to be a father.

If I had a child with Dr. Boy he would love her, to be sure, but she would never really be our child, she would be his child and she would be my child, shuttling between worlds, male and female, black and white, Christian and Jew. I didn't want that. I didn't want her to think that her father hadn't loved her mother enough to settle down and have a real family. And I didn't want her to think that I'd used getting pregnant as some desperate attempt to hang on to a relationship with a man that was going nowhere. I wanted her to be born out of desire, not heated passion between man and woman but the pure, basic need of a mother for a child. She would not be a child born of loss but a child born into plenty. She would not be born of unprotected sex, by accident; no, my daughter would be chosen again and again and again. My first choice, and only.

I didn't need Dr. Boy to be happy. And I certainly didn't need him to have a baby. By the time I left him in Texas, I had an apartment and a plan.

9.

I HELD THE BABY against my chest. He was heavy and warm and when he began to stir I stood up and bounced him a little, walking around the living room and showing him the bookcases that lined the walls. This was our time, the sun and the world barely awake, the first cups of coffee brewing in the kitchen. I thought, if only I could stay here forever, holding a three-month-old in my arms, watching him suck a dream nipple in his sleep.

Max's parents, my friends, were asleep upstairs. On my way back from the bathroom, I'd found Aimee in the nursery, changing the baby's diaper. She was in boxer shorts and a long T-shirt, wet, I'd supposed from milk. She picked him up, and he grabbed a fistful of her dark hair.

"Why don't you let me take him? You can go back to sleep."

"It's okay...I'll give him to Rich. Did he wake you?" She'd managed to extricate her hair from Max's grasp, and he peered over her shoulder at me with a look that Aimee called the "fuck you" stare. It was a look I knew well; he'd clearly inherited it from his mother.

"Oh, no," I said, "just needed to pee. But, really, I'll take him. Rich doesn't look like he's gotten a lot of sleep either."

The corners of Aimee's mouth turned up in something resembling a smile, and she passed the baby to me. I settled Max on my shoulder, supporting his head, and took him down to the living room. The wooden stairs creaked as I walked, sunlight streaking in through the blinds. My footsteps were tentative;

the last time I'd carried a baby down a flight of stairs I'd been in high school, babysitting the kids down the street. I had visions of falling and dropping him, his little skull splitting against the step. I clutched him tighter. Max cooed and drooled on my neck.

We settled on the couch, Max resting face down on my chest with my hand stroking his back and the top of his head. He sighed a little baby sigh and went back to sleep. At three months, he was heavier than my cats, warm and solid against my chest. The last time I'd seen him, after I'd gotten back from Texas, he'd had that breakable look of new babies who can't yet hold up their heads, with wide alien eyes and a turned up nose. He was funny looking, and I was bored just looking at him, and I wondered if that meant I really didn't want a baby after all. Now I thought he was the most beautiful baby I'd ever seen. I sniffed the top of his head. He smelled like milk and Johnson's baby shampoo and something earthy I couldn't name. I closed my eyes and breathed.

"He used to curl up like that all the time, when we first brought him home from the hospital." Rich interrupted my reverie. "He hasn't done it for while."

I tried to smile.

"You want some coffee? Aimee's getting dressed."

"Sure, thanks."

"If he gets heavy, just put him in the infant seat." Rich tapped the top of Max's head and smoothed the wisp of white-blonde hair. "You can still see the mark from the suction cup from when he was born."

"Hmm," I said, in agreement, though I really couldn't see anything. Aimee hadn't really talked to me about the birth, just said that he'd gotten stuck somehow and had developed an infection, and I didn't think I should ask. My mother wouldn't even really talk with me about what happened when I was born; I figured if I wasn't entitled to my own story, I probably shouldn't ask about someone else's. Besides, what would I tell her, that I'd dreamed the whole thing while I bled all over my bathroom floor?

All weekend, as we pushed Max from here to there in his stroller—peering in store windows at bedroom sets and hand-woven baskets and cinnamon scented candlesticks and sitting in the local café sipping coffee like we once had in graduate school— Aimee had a glazed, faraway look in her eyes. She didn't say much—asked a few questions about my new job, mumbled a few words about the day she went into labor—and I thought her becoming a mother felt like the thing that would finally separate us for good.

If I could have excised Rich from the family photos, Aimee's life, I thought, was exactly what I wanted. She had a Victorian house in a lovely urban neighborhood, a quick walk from coffee shops and parks, upscale restaurants and the campus where both she and Rich taught. She had a son who would grow up and play catch in their front yard and walk to the elementary school a few short blocks from their house, and she would watch him out the front window or hold his hand when he crossed the street. She had all the outward markers of happiness in American culture, and I'd never seen a person look so sad and out of place. She reminded me of Dodo Conway, pushing her baby carriage down the street in Plath's novel *The Bell Jar.* I wanted to put her and Max in my car and drive away where the three of us could live somewhere and I could hold him like that every day. I had to admit I missed her more than I missed Dr. Boy.

"You still want one?" Aimee said, as we walked Max around the block. It was my turn to push the stroller, and I looked down at Max sleeping, little baby sunglasses shading his eyes. He was wearing the onesie I'd mailed right after he was born, with a bunny and a carrot on the front. I'd spent about an hour going through Gymboree and the Children's Place and the Baby Gap, until I'd found something I thought Aimee would like.

"Yeah, I do," I said. I let out a long breath. I'd wondered when we would start talking for real, like we used to, or if that was impossible now.

When she'd called me when he was born, she sounded high on pain medication. "I highly recommend it," she'd said that night. "I haven't slept in like three months," she said now, with a heavy sigh. "All we do is sit around and watch television and feed him and change him and hold him. He screams if we put him down. I have no idea how we're going back to work. I mean, Rich is going in to the office already, and I can't even figure out where to put the baby when I pee. But I wouldn't trade him for anything." Whether she added that last sentence for my benefit or her own I really couldn't tell. "So when are you planning on having this kid?"

"I keep going back and forth. Probably next spring. I mean, I'd really like to be pregnant now, but I think it makes sense to wait a little while, until I'm settled in Texas and the job and everything." I tipped the front wheels of Max's stroller to get him up over a curb.

"You're pretty good at that," Aimee said, and she sounded genuinely impressed. "Let's go around once more and head back. Almost time for a feeding." Max began to stir in his stroller, fists flailing the summer air.

Back at the house, Rich fussed with a videotape of the baby at the hospital while Aimee prepared a bottle of breastmilk for him to drink. As my last act before heading back to Indiana, I had the honors of feeding the baby. I bounced him a little in the kitchen, holding him in the crook of my arm like a cloth-covered football. He was so hungry he rooted and clamped onto my bicep, sucking so hard he bruised the skin.

"Hey little guy, there's no milk in there," I chuckled.

"Okay, all set," Aimee said, holding the bottle up like an Olympic torch. "Why don't we go into the living room?"

I sat down with Max propped up in my arm.

"Here you go." Aimee popped the nipple in his mouth. The

top wasn't screwed on tight enough; milk dribbled onto my wrist.

"Aimee," Rich and I said simultaneously.

She tipped the bottle higher, and the milk flooded Max's onesie, the couch cushions, me. It was sweet and sticky on my arm. Through years of friendship—going to the gym in stained sweats at 7:00 a.m., talks about menstrual cramps and ovarian cysts, late nights watching television in her downstairs apartment—we'd never been this intimate, milk from her breasts wet on my shirt like I was the one lactating. In the background, pictures of Aimee in a wheelchair and bathrobe, Max in an incubator with a tube up his nose, flashed on the TV screen. Aimee gave Rich the "fuck you" stare and turned to me, the skin of her face tinged green.

"I can't watch this," Aimee said, as she undid the flap of her nursing bra put Max to her breast to drink. "Rich, please."

I excused myself and went upstairs to change my shirt.

It's been five years now, and I still can't explain what happened that weekend. I can tell you where we went and what we did and that I felt just awful, my uterus was a tight fist and the headache swam up between my eyes and over my eyebrows and then settled in my right temple where it pulsed, steadily, and I thought about the squinch owl in *The Sound and the Fury*, that if migraine had a shape that would be it. And I know that not long after that weekend, Aimee and I stopped speaking. I would write emails and send birthday cards and not hear back and eventually I just assumed that she'd made up her mind that we were no longer friends.

I thought about Aimee and Max and Rich on the drive back to Indiana on I-70. The next time I'd take that road I'd be going west, not east, headed to Texas with my cats in their carriers in the backseat, driving away from graduate school, from the life I'd shared with Aimee and our small circle of eccentric friends. Aimee was married with a baby, and I had a tenure track job. We'd grown up, it seemed.

Part II

1.

CROSSING INTO TEXAS from Oklahoma was like driving into a Steinbeck novel, peaches and watermelons in a halo of flies by the side of the road. It was beastly hot, hot enough that I burned my hand touching the hood of the car when we stopped at a gas station. The cats, one of whom had howled most of the thirteen-hour drive, had settled into summer sleep in their carriers. And my mother, who was in the passenger seat for this last stretch of the journey, demanded that we put on another CD. All my music sounded the same, she said. Paula Cole's "Where Have All the Cowboys Gone" accompanied us as we crossed the border. Something in my ovary twitched, and I wondered if there would ever come a time that I wasn't hyper-aware of my ovaries. I was fecund.

The apartment, which, when I put down my security deposit back in May, had seemed so grown-up and sophisticated compared to my beat-up one bedroom in Indiana, now seemed cheap, with slate blue carpet that was barely tacked down and still damp from chemical cleaning, and pressed-wood cabinets in the kitchen and bathroom. I tossed the keys on the kitchen counter, settled the cats' carriers next to the fireplace I was sure I'd never use, and unpacked the handful of boxes Mom had meticulously arranged, like a 3D jigsaw puzzle, back in my apartment parking lot in Indiana. I gave her the name Master Packer and brought the single box that didn't fit to the post office, mailing it to myself. I'd never seen anything like it; even the pockets in the doors were put to use, holding doodads and lone earrings that had turned up under my bed after the movers hauled it away. Now, in this strange new world, Dannon nestled into one of the book boxes from the car, while Pistachio, the larger of the two cats, wedged herself in the four inch space between the refrigerator and the wall in fear, her back legs and tail facing out. The moving truck wouldn't be here with the rest of my stuff for days. I took a tour of my empty rooms. I turned on the water and flushed the toilet. I sighed.

I had a headache. I wanted to go home.

As always, Mom had a shopping list, so we headed into town. On the square, across the street from the county courthouse, we found a furniture store—three floors of massive four-poster beds and tables with seating for twelve and oversized couches with green upholstery. Everything about Texas seemed too large and unmanageable for me to grasp. (What had Lee said before I left? Don't mess with Texas.) But I needed furniture—I'd abandoned a repeatedly-used Goodwill couch in the old apartment (they charged me more to haul it away than I'd paid to buy it in the first place), and in my first decision as going-to-be-mom, I decided I was renouncing the hand-me-down twin bed I'd inherited when a friend got married for a mahogany sleigh bed I'd been coveting for months—so we took our first steps across the threshold.

I was scared. Like most things, selecting furniture struck me as some kind of profound metaphor for adult life. Mom followed me as I walked from bedroom set to bedroom set, kitchen table to kitchen table, oversized sofa to oversized sofa. We'd gone through the same sighing and hand wringing when I wrote the check for the down payment on my new car. She told me, more bemused than annoyed, that I'd done the same thing as a child, figuring out the best way to spend my birthday money by walking the aisles of Toys 'R' Us; there were so many life-sized plastic dolls to choose from! For a long time, I stood in front of a big sleigh bed—similar to the piece Lee dubbed the "bed of dreams" but not exactly right—unable make up my mind if I could settle for not exactly right. But I also needed some place to sleep. So I paced from room to room in the over air-conditioned store, my hair high in a pony tail, an old flannel shirt over my tank top and the cut-offs from my favorite pair of high school jeans. This whole process took so long that I even annoyed myself. The sales clerk followed me around, pretending to tidy up arrangements of fake flowers or fluff pillows housed on the mammoth beds. I could hear the click clack of her heels. I wondered how long she would follow me, before she just gave up.

It was a slow day at the store; the thermometer on the bank read 103 degrees, and I imagined everyone else in town more or less naked in their homes with the AC blasting. I'd sunburned just walking down the street after we'd parked our car a few blocks away; eventually I would learn to keep sunscreen in the glove compartment. I think we must have been the only customers in the store. The clerk caught up to us next to the not-quite-bed-of-dreams and started to make polite, I'm-on-commission small talk.

"Hello. Welcome to Queen's Furniture. I'm Eliza Jane. Can I help you find something?"

"Thank you. I'm just looking around." I tucked a loose strand of hair back behind my ears and remembered to smile.

"This is a beautiful bedroom set for a master bedroom," she gushed, like she was just seeing it for the first time. "We're having a special on mattresses. This is a good time to buy." She flipped the price tag on the bed over so I could see it.

"That's good to know, thanks."

"Are you looking for anything else?"

"Couch. Kitchen table." I put my hands in my pockets and looked over at Mom. "I just moved down here," I added.

"How wonderful! I've lived here for fifteen years and just love it. Everyone's so friendly."

I nodded. I'd about used up my friendliness quotient for the day and it was only 10:30.

"Did your husband just get transferred down here, honey?" she asked.

I didn't follow how she assumed a young woman sporting a ponytail and walking around with someone who was obviously her mother must have been married and unemployed, but that was only one of many things I didn't understand about my introduction to Small Town Texas.

"Actually," I said, carefully, "I just got a job at the college."

"Well, well. It's a great place. A lot of my friends do clerical work in the administration building. What will you be doing?"

"I'm a professor of English."

"Oh. I see." There was something like contempt in her voice. "Well, it's a very nice community. Have you found a church yet? I'd be happy to give you the name of mine."

I needed to get her away from my mother and her overworked anti-Semitic radar. She was already a little skeptical that I'd taken a job at a college with a vague religious affiliation. The first thing she looked up in the phone book was the number for the synagogue, the closest of which was in the big city an hour away. I smiled. "Maybe you could point me in the direction of your kitchen tables?"

I didn't have a husband. And most of the time I didn't consider this fact a problem but one of my better qualities. Frankly, I didn't know anyone who had a good marriage. My parents had divorced when I was four, and then my mother remarried and divorced again when I was twenty-one. So I had a father and an ex-stepfather, and, at the moment, I wasn't speaking to either one of them, for reasons even I wasn't sure I could artic-ulate. All my married friends did was badmouth their spouses, except for Aimee, who couldn't even decide when to nurse the baby without consulting Rich. Now she even watched football on TV. Visiting her had only solidified my belief that having a child without all the nonsense of heterosexual partnership was the way to go. It did occur to me that maybe I was just deluding myself, that maybe the problem wasn't marriage as an institution but that I couldn't find someone I was remotely interested in marrying, or who was remotely interested in marrying me. Then again, I didn't really try. It was just easier and more pleasant to spend Saturday nights watching a movie with a girlfriend than putting on lipstick, shaving my legs, and making idle conversation in a smoky bar.

I don't think the reality of Texas hit me until the lock snicked shut when my mother left for the airport and I was alone with beige walls and new carpet smell. I had just gotten here, hadn't even met all of my colleagues yet, and was already coming up with the plan to leave. In the second bedroom, the one I imagined would become a nursery someday, I sat at my desk—the dark cherry table that my grandparents had once used for dinner parties—doing something that resembled work. My uncle had carved his name there, as a child, and in another corner my ex-stepfather had left scratchings of numbers as he did our taxes one year. I thumbed through a stack of poems that were becoming my first adult manuscript, "The Baby Book," and I rearranged some paragraphs of a conference paper due in a few weeks. But the real issue wasn't one that could be easily researched in a library. How to find the father of the baby of your dreams.

I could see her so clearly, this child with dark curly hair. When I pictured the scene, it was almost always spring, her new white sandals resting against my hip as I held her. She wore a light cotton sweater (also white), one of her chubby hands playing with the neckline of my shirt or my hair. Her skin was darker than mine, the color of coffee or the light brown M&M candies from my childhood. I thought about sex and Punnett squares, all the permutations of genes that could make such a beautiful child. And I thought, this is the daughter I could have with Dr. Boy.

But having a baby with Dr. Boy was out of the question. That much I'd decided when I visited him in May. Oh, he was happy enough to have sex on occasion but any more than that sent him running in fear. And the logistics of trying to get pregnant with a gay friend—a "known donor"—seemed virtually impossible. All this, of course, was hypothetical, since I hadn't asked, but I wasn't going to ask unless I was really darn sure that "yes" would be the desirable outcome. That left what was neat, clean, simple. Anonymous donor. Immaculate conception of the twenty-first century.

These were the things that I thought about as I sat at my desk and then, when night began to fall, walked laps around my new apartment complex, watching grasshoppers mate next to parked Ford trucks. The parking lot was blanketed with them, like a plague from the Old Testament. All summer my nerves had sizzled into migraine headaches and heart palpitations, jittery with anticipation of the life I hadn't yet started to live. Even now, with the boxes unpacked and new, grown-up furniture filling the open rooms, I couldn't move quickly enough. I walked. A girl tugged her brother around the parking lot, carrying a suitcase in her other hand. A woman holding a cigarette watched them from a patio in the distance, and I wondered if she was their mother. I wondered if they were running away.

On the radio that morning, the woman who used to play Blair on that eighties sitcom *The Facts of Life* prattled on about Jesus Christ, A-men. And my apartment sat in the shadow of the big white cross of the Harvest of God-or-Something-or-Other church next door. I lived in Texas now, and I was damned. To what, I wasn't sure.

I was pulled toward the city. The highway was exactly four miles from the apartment down the winding farm road where I lived, a road that curved around so it went both north and west. Driving south, the highway stretched ahead in an endless line of orange cones and concrete blockades. Even then, the symbolism struck me as blatantly obvious: the highway and the journey to new life, the seemingly tangible barrier between small town provincialism and the illusory liberalism of the big city. Getting on that highway, a native North Texan once told me, was like crossing the Mason Dixon line. I was pulled to the city even though by nature I'd rather be at home, reading in an overstuffed chair. I was drawn to the city like a tiny magnet to a big hunk of metal. Whatever I needed, I knew I would find there.

My favorite place in all of Texas was the Whole Foods. I found it my first week there, an hour on the highway I would eventually travel up and down for more hours than I care to remember, singing along to Avril Lavigne's moody "Life's Like This" on the radio. On the same corner there was Whole Foods and Starbucks, Borders and Barnes and Noble, and soon enough I'd find the Babies 'R' Us and the Old Navy that carried maternity clothes. My best students could have written a doozy of a cultural analysis on what drew me there—the color of the paint on the walls, the arrangement of the aisles, the height of the items on the shelves—but in the most basic terms, I was homesick and I found comfort in recognizable brand names and store chains. More than that, a familiar suburban middle class lifestyle rooted in the produce section—it felt like the town I'd grown up in, plus organic sweet potatoes. Pregnant women pushing shopping carts. Toddlers in Hanna Andersson knits. Young men holding apples to their noses and mulling over the difference between gala and braeburn. The daughter I hadn't conceived yet knocked on my ovary. An imaginary son tugged on my leg. I bought blood oranges and kalamata olives, baby spinach and new asparagus. I sat with my grocery bags, sipping coffee in the café, watching mothers nurse their babies under blankets, trying to be discrete. All I could think was, I want that.

After I couldn't justify sitting any longer, I loaded up the hot car with perishables layered between bags of ice. I threaded through side streets until I found the highway headed north.

My heart raced with the car's engine. If I drove far enough, I'd go past my apartment, past Oklahoma and all of Missouri and end up home. My mother would be waiting for me with chicken and potatoes in the oven, with clean sheets on the bed. She would light candles, like she did sometimes on holidays, and my siblings would come over to eat. We would talk and play Scrabble until late in the night and have homemade waffles for breakfast in the morning. We would listen to NPR and discuss our choices for presidential candidates.

Who was I kidding? I said my family lived in Chicago, but I wasn't sure what that meant anymore. I left home when I was seventeen and hadn't really looked back. When I watched the station wagon pull away that first day at college and then, again, my first day at graduate school, I felt only relief, like the first deep breath after an asthma attack. Finally, I found a place where I belonged, a place I chose, a place that chose me, not a family I was tied to just because, years ago, my mother had sex with my father. That first day I unpacked my collections of poetry and a closet full of black clothes and went to the bookstore to stock up on pens and legal pads before heading downstairs for the cafeteria with my new friends and the boy who, in a few weeks, would become my first love. Still, all I had to do was get on a bus or a train and two hours later I'd be home, in my own room with a walk-in closet where I hid and wrote stories, sitting on a pile of shoes.

Now I felt cut off from everything I knew. My mother, tending her marigolds and peonies; late night drives with whichever of my siblings had gotten into trouble; adventures with Lee who had moved to California for school. Even Dr. Boy who was only an hour away. Still, I had to admit my fantasies of family were much more striking than the reality. I needed to invent a new one, here in Texas.

2.

THE SHIFT FROM SUMMER TO FALL was so subtle I wouldn't have noticed it, except for the fact that I was now expected to show up to classes and faculty meetings. It was still unbearably hot, the kind of heat that frizzled my hair and left rings of perspiration on my underwear. I wore my Ann Taylor dresses with bare legs and chunky-soled sandals, though I needed layers of sweaters to sit through new faculty orientation, and my fingers still turned blue from the air conditioning. I made photocopies. I alphabetized my books. I figured out how to change the height on my swiveling desk chair.

I tried out all the restaurants in town. I tried what the Texans called chili, which really wasn't chili, just ground meat in spiced tomato sauce served with a side order of tortilla chips and guacamole. I tried catfish and chicken fried steak. I tried drinking iced tea instead of Coke. I learned to smile when my new colleagues stopped me on the quad to chat about the latest bookstore mishap and to ask how I liked it in Texas so far.

Everyone was impossibly nice, but I couldn't yet consider anyone a true friend. I needed someone like Aimee or Lee, someone I could pal around with, someone to watch videos with on quiet Friday nights, someone to call when the cat decided to hide and I thought she was missing, someone I could invite over for dinner and wear pajamas or a pair of beat up gray sweatpants that had followed me from college and not feel like I was being judged.

Dr. Boy was an hour away, doing his own thing. I needed to find mine.

What I found, eventually, was a yoga class, tucked in the far corner of a three-story building on the square that mostly housed lawyers' offices and boutiques that sold pottery and things carved out of wood. Joanna, the owner, had three small rooms, one that doubled as a waiting area and a yoga studio, one that served her massage clients, and one for her partner's use.

My first yoga class in Texas was a lot like my first bowl of chili in Texas. I could see the family resemblance but it was far from what I expected.

For starters, there were too many of us crammed into the small room. We needed to move wooden benches and tables into the small corridor to set our mats on the floor. The mats were those pink and blue vinyl mats that kindergarteners used for nap, and I tried not to be disappointed before the class even began. I was used to a large dance studio in a large student recreation facility. I was used to taking classes with graduate students and faculty who decided they needed to do something about the stresses of academic life. Today I was, unquestionably, the youngest person in the room. The other students were graying grandmotherly types—middle-aged, middle-class women with enough disposable income for luxuries like massage therapy and yoga. The cars parked outside were Lexuses and BMWs, far from the Ford trucks that lined the parking spaces outside my apartment complex. These women looked like they could be my mother's friends.

This wasn't what I pictured at all.

The class was too slow and too fast all at once. Joanna, a tall woman with long flowing pants and top, moved gracefully though a series of poses to the rhythm of breath. From cat to cow to cat again and cat to cobra to cat to child. We didn't stay in any pose longer than a single breath. I wanted to slow down. I wanted to keep my body still and relax into each posture, to feel each of my muscles stretch and open, to embrace the challenge and soreness. And I wanted to go faster, to be in a class for more advanced students. At the end of that first class, I tallied up all the poses we hadn't done: down dog and up dog, shoulder stand, and the bridge pose I so loved.

I was a creature of habit. I didn't want anything to change.

My first semester came and went in a seemingly endless string of student papers and faculty meetings. Five days a week, I taught my classes and sat in my Texas-sized office chatting with students and writing up discussion questions for the novels we read. My office was in a low-traffic hallway on the third floor of a small office building, and my colleagues joked that students only came up there if they really wanted to talk. When I needed a break, I'd walk across the tree-lined quad to the student union and get a free cup of coffee or apple juice, one of the faculty perks. I checked my campus mail in the small post office, where students picked up care packages and hung up flyers for parties and one-act plays, hoping, like they did I supposed, for a letter from someone who loved me, Aimee or Lee or my grandfather. More often than not, my box held only the agendas for upcoming faculty meetings and papers students dared to submit late, with Post-Its that read "Thanks for understanding!"

Through October and November and into December, I waited for the leaves to turn colors and fall into bright piles on the sidewalk. I waited for the days to become mostly nights, for the air to become so cold I could take out my charcoal colored coat and the purple and turquoise scarf Lee had given me for my last birthday. I waited for my body to adjust to the rhythms of Texas, to the sound of the air conditioning units outside my window, to the slivers of light the mini blinds made on the carpet in the bedroom. All semester long, I waited.

At night, when all the meetings were done, when I'd gone over my notes and made my copies for the next day's lesson, when the students filed to the cafeteria for hamburgers and frozen yogurt, I headed home to my apartment on the outskirts of town, as close to the city as I could get without heading down the highway.

In the evenings I cooked or went to yoga class and then ended up on the couch with the cats, reading novels for class and wishing for noise. From my living room window, I could see my neighbors getting their mail or lugging plastic baskets to the laundry center. It felt like I was watching a version of *Melrose Place* in which the largest drama was figuring out who owned the Japanese car in the parking lot or who didn't put an American flag out after September 11. Sometimes I had dinner with other new faculty or a group of colleagues who always met Friday nights at 7:00 at a locally owned restaurant. We chatted amicably about our favorite students and their plans for study abroad or trips to the city to go to the theater. I listened to the clink of wine glasses and the room swollen with laughter and felt myself shrink in the booth. I wondered if I would ever feel like I belonged, or if I would always feel like the new kid in the class. None of it seemed real.

I could count on one hand the times Dr. Boy drove up and we had dinner, or I drove to see him and we lounged around his new apartment with armchairs that I told him looked like dorm furniture, even though he was now living on a professor's salary. Once I would have loved him for that, back in the days we romanticized poverty and ate ramen cooked in the residence hall kitchen on Sunday nights instead of the quaint café across the street. Now it served as a reminder that even though we lived, again, in the same state, we were never so far apart, the distance between us longer than the miles of the farm roads between here and there. There was always a reason he didn't visit—he had to write, he had to read, he didn't have enough money for gas. Even now, I don't think he knew how lonely I was.

When I turned in my grades for the semester, I sat down with the handbook from my insurance company and started calling the fertility specialists in the area. I imagined what the second bedroom would look like as a nursery instead of an office. I imagined what my nights would be like as a mother, putting the baby down in a room with alphabet blocks painted on the walls, sitting in a rocking chair in the corner while she sucked her chubby hands until she fell asleep. Then I'd go into the kitchen and wash up the dinner dishes, and settle on the couch with a basket of laundry waiting to be folded. The cats would join me, resting their gray and white heads on clean towels and crib sheets, waiting for me to stroke their ears. And after the apartment settled into the quiet of night, I'd check on the sleeping baby, brush my teeth, and, for the first time in my life, fall easily, peacefully, to sleep.

3.

THE HIGHWAY WAS LONG. The crotch of my black suit pants was all sweaty, and I was dreading the fact that the doctor was, I was sure, going to ask me to strip. Sooner or later, she was going to ask me to take off my clothes, put on one of those godawful paper gowns, lie down on the table and open my legs. It was like the first time with a new lover. On the passenger seat sat the fifteen-page questionnaire the receptionist I would soon come to adore had sent me, after bending the rules to make sure that I got a female doctor even though she didn't technically work with single patients anymore. If I was going to conceive a child without the help of a husband, I wasn't going to do it with a man at all. That much I knew.

The highway was too long. There was an accident halfway between here and there, and the drivers of the Ford trucks who knew where they were going made U-turns and took the frontage road the other direction. I drummed my hands on the steering wheel and sighed. I just hoped that I didn't make this new doctor mad.

I hated being late more than I hated other people being late.

I'd flagged the appointment in huge pink letters in my planner. The minute class ended that afternoon, I gathered my books and bolted out of class before the students had an opportunity to ask me questions. Usually, I lingered, talking about this and that, the new film about Sylvia Plath or the coffee shop that had finally opened downtown. Everything I'd thought of for more than a year, since that night I'd talked to Dr. Boy on the phone, led up to this moment. If my life were a short story I taught my students, this ride on the highway would be the climax, the point to which everything rises and then descends. But life is rarely as neat and patterned as a short story.

I felt like I was going on a blind date. I wondered if the doctor would be pretty. I decided she would be very pretty and very young. I decided she was a lesbian who devoted her life to helping other lesbians and unmarried women and couples with reproductive problems get pregnant. I was glad I'd taken the time that morning to shave my legs.

As I sat in traffic, I studied the buildings that lined the highway. Restaurants with flashing neon signs and motels that featured weekly rates. Right on the outskirts of the city I was greeted by a major construction site, flanked by orange cones and a church with a huge cross. The cars began to speed up again. I studied my directions and looked for my exit, panic like wings flapping in my chest.

I hated driving. I hadn't gotten my driver's license until I was a freshman in college, and only then because my ex-stepfather had forced me and paid for private driving lessons. I told myself that if I couldn't even drive to a new place, I certainly wasn't ready to be a mother. Lately I'd been telling myself that every time I confronted something I didn't really want to do. It worked pretty well as a motivational strategy.

I found my turn-off. On the right was a college that had sent me books via interlibrary loan. If I craned my neck, I could see the football stadium tucked back behind a strip mall. That had to be a good sign. I sat in more traffic, weaving through the streets of the university and the expensive houses that only doctors and lawyers and Texas oil families could afford. One had an elephant fountain in front, with water dribbling out of its trunk into a pond. And just past the university, there was an outdoor shopping mall that touted valet parking. I was simultaneously drawn in and repulsed.

Despite the construction and traffic and getting a late start,

I made my way up to the fertility specialist's office just a few minutes late, handing a nameless parking attendant my keys so I didn't need to worry about finding a parking space and walking around campus. The clinic was on the fifth floor of a large medical center, flanked by two larger, university-affiliated hospitals and classroom buildings, with laboratories and lecture halls for the medical school. I checked myself in at the front desk, writing my name and the time of my appointment with a shaky, sweaty hand. In the waiting room, I sat with women who were pregnant or not, flipped through pages of parenting magazines, and opened my backpack repeatedly to make sure my questionnaire and old medical records were still safely tucked inside. When I left my apartment, I went through a similar ritual of saying "off, off, off, off" to each of the burners on the stove. The compulsiveness, I thought, was one of my least attractive qualities. I made sure the pages of the questionnaire were in the right order, and put them in my backpack. On the television, a doctor was being interviewed about the importance of folic acid in early pregnancy.

Eventually, a nurse wearing blue scrubs called my name. She escorted me from the waiting area to the row of examination and procedure rooms. She weighed me and took my height. She recorded my temperature, pulse, and blood pressure on a crisp new chart. Then she showed me in to a nondescript office with beige walls where the doctor sat behind a desk, like someone else's secretary, fiddling with the gold charm at her throat. I was right. She was beautiful, her long blond hair pulled back in a sleek black headband.

There was a plastic container filled with her business cards. Dr. Catherine Williams, Clinical Assistant Professor, Reproductive Endocrinology and Infertility. I think she must have introduced herself. I think I shook her hand. I put my backpack on the chair beside me and sat down. My heart was racing, like it did the day I took my Ph.D. qualifying exams. I supposed this test was equally important.

The woman I would later describe to my friends as Dr. Cathexis, or the Divine Dr. C, flipped through the pages of my chart, clearing her throat at regular intervals.

"You're twenty-nine," Dr. Williams said, "and you want to do artificial insemination?"

I parsed her words. I was an English professor. Unraveling sentences was what I did best. I wanted to tell her that "want" was one of those words I wasn't sure I would use but, yes, I wanted to have a baby and this seemed like the best way to do it. I also wanted to tell her that, even though she was the expert on human reproduction, "artificial insemination" was neither a socially acceptable nor medically useful term.

I must have made a face. My professors had always told me in graduate school that my face gave me away.

She blushed. "Sometimes the nurses use the term 'IUI-AD' to refer to intrauterine insemination with an anonymous donor."

I smiled.

I think she must have asked me why, or perhaps I just launched into my readymade speech about Dr. Boy and being more certain about this hypothetical baby than I'd ever been certain about anything, including graduate school and the job that had landed me in this huge southern state, and eventually in her office.

She said something vague about motherhood being hard, and I couldn't tell if she spoke from experience. "I mean, what would you do if the baby got sick?"

"I guess I'd call the pediatrician. Figure out if I needed to stay home with her, if she could go to daycare. I imagine it would depend what was wrong with her, right?"

"What about your job? Being a university professor isn't easy. How will you negotiate the demands of single motherhood and full-time employment?"

Defensiveness puffed up my chest like a balloon. I imagined it deflating with a cartoon "pop" before I spoke. "Well, I think one of the great things about my job is its flexibility. If I had to, I could cancel class and stay home. From what I can tell, the college is a really family friendly environment." The voice that came out of my mouth was my interview voice, overly confident, like I'd been given a copy of the questions beforehand.

If she'd asked me what I thought new motherhood was like, I would have described my fantasy: straightening up the apartment while the baby slept and then sitting in the rocking chair and nursing her when she woke up.

"You're twenty-nine," I think she must have said again.

"Is that okay with you?" I'd assumed because of her job she had to be a feminist, at least in the way I taught my reluctant students about feminism, a basic demand for equality between men and women. I'd assumed she needed to be liberal, to see the possibilities of human coupling and reproduction that the very nature of her work allowed. It honestly never occurred to me that she would have been anything other than likeminded.

"I just want you to understand what you're getting into. You're so young."

That was what everyone said when I told them I was thinking about having a baby. Some variation on you're so young, what if you meet a great guy? or why now? or why don't you wait until you have tenure? All these questions told me was how little my desires resembled those of other women my age, or how frightened most single women were of not finding a partner and how culturally expected marriage was. Even women I'd chatted with online, women who were also thinking about becoming single moms, encouraged me to wait, date a little, keep single motherhood in mind as a backup plan; how could it possibly be my first choice?

"I think I'd like to have two children. I think I'd like to have them about five years apart. So starting to try now seems like a good idea, right?" I was vaguely annoyed. I shouldn't have to explain to a fertility specialist what she must have told women all the time: after your twenties fertility begins to decline, after thirty-five it drops sharply, after forty there's not much chance at all. If I knew what I wanted, why should I risk losing it just because it made some people squeamish to think about women raising kids without husbands?

She smiled tenderly. "Sounds like you've given this a lot of thought."

"Yeah. It's pretty much all I think about."

I guess I convinced her I was psychologically stable, because she started drawing diagrams on sheets of paper about what a woman's menstrual cycle looks like and the pills she wanted me to start taking and the host of tests she wanted to do before we proceeded.

"I wanted to try natural cycles," I interjected when she started saying words like "Clomid" and "injectables" and "HCG shots."

"Well, sure, there's no reason to think you have any fertility problems at this point, but donor sperm is quite expensive, and if I were you I'd want to up my chances of conception."

"But I'm only twenty-nine," I found myself protesting. I was at a fertility clinic. I supposed it only made sense that I'd get treated like a real fertility patient.

"Well, let's go check you over. Your last exam was about a year ago?"

Seamlessly, she walked me across the hall where another nurse in blue scrubs handed me a paper gown. The doctor disappeared for a phone call with another doctor, while I folded my sweaty suit and laid it on the chair, along with my backpack. I barely had time to hop back on to the table and cover myself with a white sheet when she knocked on the door. This is what she did all day, moving from conversations on the phone to standing between women's legs, searching for what we didn't ourselves know was there. Babies and cancers, freckles and skin tags. Her eyes were on my face while her hands read my body like Braille, the swell of my breasts and the cave of my uterus. I've often thought if I had to have another career, helping women have babies would be a good one.

"I think you're ovulating," she pronounced, sticking the long cotton swab in a plastic container to send to the lab, muttering something about cervical fluid and the position of the cervix.

"Oh," I thought, it all begins now.

"What do you do for exercise?" she asked.

"I'm taking a yoga class."

"Do you like it? I've been doing Pilates. I find it a little more intense."

I couldn't tell if she was being friendly or if these questions were part of the interview she was doing, to figure out if I was ready to be a mom—body and mind and soul.

When I was dressed again, I met her back in the sterile office and she checked off a list of tests on a requisition form. She wanted to test hormone levels and immunity to disease, blood type and thyroid function. She wanted to shoot dye in my uterus and take an x-ray, to see if my fallopian tubes were open. There were all kinds of acronyms and insurance codes, a new lexicon I wanted desperately to understand. She said to take the papers to the lab upstairs and to talk to her nurse when I'd picked a donor was ready to get started trying. It seemed unfathomable. Only a year ago I'd been absolutely crazed, giving birth to blood clots in my tub.

As I said goodbye to her, I felt the ping of ovulation in my left side. A normal woman who wanted to get pregnant would find her husband or boyfriend and have sex. I went upstairs to the ninth floor to have my blood drawn.

4.

I FELL IN LOVE with the chemistry Ph.D. He was five- feet-eleven inches in height and weighed one-hundred-eighty pounds. His favorite food was pad thai and he had four cats. No allergies as a child. His maternal grandparents were Russian Jews. His paternal grandparents were Irish immigrants. All four had lived into their nineties and died of what he termed "natural" causes. He had two older sisters. In his essay, he wrote that he wanted to donate sperm because his eldest sister had struggled with infertility, and he wanted to give every woman who wanted a child a chance to have one. He also wasn't sure whether he wanted to marry and have children himself. In ten years, he saw himself working in a lab developing a cure for ovarian cancer. He swam every day and hoped to do a triathlon someday. I imagined a child with his aptitude for the hard sciences and my artistic sentiment and sighed.

I ruled out donors who said that their favorite animals were dogs, hearty American men who preferred hamburgers to Indian cuisine. More logical friends told me that I wasn't picking a spouse or even a date, just a vial of sperm. Intelligence, a family history of good health and mental stability, and good motility should be top priorities. Nothing else really mattered. I rationalized my haphazard methodology with the thought that in the "real world" it is these quirky, personal things, like favorite animals and foods, that go into dating, and in turn into mating, which is, after all, what I was doing. I was just cutting out the small talk and the need to shave my legs, though in the end, I ended up doing both, just for a pretty doctor instead of a prospective lover.

To be sure, there were some distinctions. In the real world I always ended up with tall men, men who towered over me by a good twelve inches, men who literally picked me up and flung me around (my friends in college played a nauseating game called Robin-ball), against all my better feminist sensibilities. Beyond that, I didn't really have a "type." I dated an ex-football player who liked Coleridge, I dated a floppy-haired boy who wrote mystery novels and listened to Depeche Mode, I dated a strawberry blonde with hair longer than mine whom I liked to call my ex-Celticist. He studied dead languages and took trips to Ireland over the summer. And then there was Dr. Boy, with his basketball player legs and his radio show voice, with the most beautiful dark chocolate skin I had ever seen. I wondered how any of them would characterize themselves on the cryobank questionnaire.

So one Friday night in April, I sat on the floor in my living room, with the donor profiles spread out in front of me like a game of cards, drinking a glass of Australian shiraz. I read and reread their short profiles, their medical histories, their essays. I put on red lipstick and old CDs, Elton John and Billy Bragg, Erasure and Pet Shop Boys, Aimee Mann and Fiona Apple, an odd collection of music inspired by the men who'd wandered in and out of my life since the age of seventeen. I turned off the lights and danced, moving my hips from side to side, thinking of the men I had once loved, men who had touched me in parked cars and rented rooms, men who had sparred with me about feminism and American politics, men with whom I had shared meals and long walks under the harvest moon, men who had never really known me. I wasn't sure if that was their fault or mine.

When I couldn't dance anymore, when I was dizzy with possibility, when the darkness was too much to bear, I took out a box of stationery and a black pen. Dear B, I wrote, Dear C,

Dear T. I wrote them all, the men I had once loved, and told them I was going to become a mom. I licked the envelopes and sealed them shut. I carried them outside, to the drop box for the post office, scraping my bare feet on the pavement. The heavy metal door on the mail box slammed shut; there was no taking the letters back.

I ran back inside and locked the door to my apartment. Then I picked up the chemist's file and held it to my lips, leaving a lipstick print next to the donor number.

I wondered, vaguely, if I would ever kiss a man again. I wondered if I would really go through with The Baby Plan. I wondered if Dr. Boy would do anything to try to stop me.

I fell asleep with the donor profiles next to me on the bed.

5.

MY STUDENTS WANTED to come over to my place for a party. I can't remember if I gave them the idea or if they came up with it on their own, but they were doing a poetry reading to celebrate the end of the semester, and I agreed that a reception for them would be very nice. The only problem was I still didn't have a table in my dining room. The tall bookcases that Dr. Boy had helped me assemble lined the walls but other than that, there was nothing in that space, just the recent absence of boxes that Dannon used to use as a climber. Sometimes I spread out my yoga mat and did some cursory stretches there. Mostly I ignored the room, except when I needed to grab a book for class.

I went back to the store where I'd bought the bedroom set, where the salesclerk had said I could join her church. I walked in quickly, past the greeter, upstairs to the second floor where they kept the kitchen and dining room furniture. It struck me as ridiculously funny that I made the decision to be a single mother in about one second flat, and it had taken me an entire school year, almost exactly the length of a pregnancy, to choose a kitchen table. I understood that I was designing the setting of a fantasy: my future daughter and I would sit at the table together, eating French toast for breakfast or me prodding her to eat her peas at dinnertime or licking ice creams with the sound of the air conditioner in the background. This table would go with us to whatever house we happened to buy. And perhaps, like my well-worn desk that was once my grandparents' dining room set, it would stay in our family for years. I was tired of assemble-it-yourself furniture, the transience of graduate school and apartment living, and piece-by-carefully-chosen-piece, I was creating a home for my child and me. Kids do homework at kitchen tables, their mothers fixing dinner in the background. Families eat at kitchen tables, coming together once or twice or three times a day for food and discussion before the teenagers run off to play practice or soccer, and the parents settle in for the night.

As I dreamed her up in the kitchen section of the furniture store, she was about two years old, in the thick of toddlerdom, strapped into a plastic booster seat, with a Mickey Mouse plate in front of her. She wore a blue T-shirt that said "Future Feminist" on the front and a pair of faded denim shorts; purple and red finger paint stains completed the ensemble. With a studied meticulousness most often reserved for science labs, she dipped French fries in ketchup and licked it off before eating the spit-coated potato. She repeated the actions over and over until she had completely emptied her plate.

"These fre fries good, Mommy!" she shrieked. "I have more?"

"Yes, honey, you can have more." The calm, mother version of me picked up her plate and walked back to the stove, where the rest of the fries lay cooling on a cookie sheet covered in foil. I gave her another handful, added another squeeze of ketchup to her plate, and sat back down next to her.

She took one of the potatoes and dipped it and then looked at my empty dish. "You no have fries, Mommy? Eat sompfing."

"I'm not hungry right now, honey. I had enough to eat."

"Have it," she said, holding out her offering, "eat more." She pushed it into my mouth, mashing it against my front teeth.

I swallowed it, baby spit and all, and I thought, this is what it means to be a mother. No one could have given a better sales pitch; I bought the table that had incited the fantasy, a Pottery Barn knockoff with a honey-colored top and cream-colored legs. It arrived the day before the party. I wiped it down with citrus-scented cleaner and put a glass vase that had once been my grandmother's in the center. My home was full.

6.

TWO BLUE LINES. I pulled the Clear Plan box out of the trash and reread the directions. Was the test line as dark or darker than the control line? Yes. Or I thought so. I'd been staring so long at the test strip that the colors had blurred into migraine; all I could think of was sitting in my high school art class mixing paint in a white plastic pallet, adding blue to white one careful drop at a time until it turned pale doctor's office blue and then true blue ribbon blue and then adding black until it darkened to night on a country road. That day, learning about color intensity and shade, the blues lined up neatly like samples of paint in the hardware store. I closed my eyes. Now I couldn't see blue anymore, just yellow starbursts and black holes.

When I opened my eyes again, I caught a fuzzy glimpse of myself in the mirror, still in my underwear and an old gray tank top speckled with holes from the cats' claws. My hair was knotted around a black elastic band. This would never do.

I dialed the number for the clinic as I debated my wardrobe choices. The orange and pink plaid pants, the ones Lee had called sherbet-colored, barely buttoned, a harbinger of weight gain to come. I paired the orange T-shirt with cream-colored linen pants, brushed my hair and put it in a respectable ponytail.

"Hi," I said when the nurse finally picked up, "I'm a patient of Dr. Williams, I got a positive on an ovulation test and need to come in today for an IUI. Yes, okay..." The nurse put me on hold again while she went to check something about sperm thawing in the lab.

I stared at the test strip on the bathroom counter. Which was the control line again? I frowned. I looked like a college student. I took my hair out of the ponytail and put on pink lipstick. Then I remembered this was June, in Texas. The air conditioner had already been on steadily for more than a month. I put my hair up again. I wondered why it mattered to me what my hair looked like or what I wore. This wasn't a date; it was just a routine medical procedure that would be billed to Blue Cross Blue Shield. I wondered what the chemist was doing while I prepared for a rendezvous with a vial of his sperm.

I stopped at the gas station just before the on ramp to the highway and filled up my gas tank. I had to admit The Baby Plan was not particularly good for the environment, or the tires on my car; it was a 70-mile drive each way, and I'd be doing it at least twice a month for the foreseeable future. The highway was not particularly scenic, either, flanked by gas stations and truck stops, restaurants and cheap motels.

On the drive, I thought about the "specimens" that I'd ordered, shipped from California in a tank of dry ice, like an alien fetus from *The X-Files*. The sample needed to be "prepared," the nurse had said, thawed and reviewed under a microscope by someone, I hoped, who had a Ph.D. in sperm preparation.

On the drive, I listened to Cher singing "A Different Kind of Love Song." I listened to Kylie Minogue singing "Can't Get You Out of My Head." Everything seemed imbued with significance, the way that my students talked about symbols, that it makes a difference if a writer chooses to have a character eat a grapes or an apple while she decides whether to have an affair with a married man.

Today, the drive took an hour and fifteen minutes, I noted in the clinic lobby. I wondered which would happen first, me getting pregnant or the completion of the highway project.

Today in my backpack I had I brought John Barth's "Life Story" with me because it seemed appropriate to read a narrative from the point of view of sperm while waiting to be inseminated. The little guys controlled everything, including the one thing I most wanted in the world.

I waited in the waiting area for an impossibly long time, trying to pay attention to the hospital show on TV. I was saving Barth for the actual procedure itself. I looked around at the other patients, sitting in their stock doctor's office chairs with mauve cushions and reading magazines. They all seemed focused intently on *Ladies Home Journal*, or *Women's Day*, or *Mothering* or whatever they were reading. No one else seemed particularly anxious. There wasn't anyone who looked like she could be pregnant, either.

I checked the clock at the receptionist's desk. My appointment was scheduled for half an hour ago. I never knew what to do in situations like this. I didn't want to be annoying, but I didn't want to sit there all day, if someone had forgotten to tell someone that I was here, waiting for what could have been the most important day of my life. I decided to give it another ten minutes.

Eventually, a tall, red-headed nurse opened the door to the waiting area and poked her head out. She looked just like Helen Reddy in *Pete's Dragon*, one of my favorite childhood movies. I decided this had to be a good sign. "Robin?"

I smiled at her and grabbed my backpack, John Barth tucked inside like a stowaway.

"Sorry to keep you waiting so long," she said, leading me down the hall. "Needed to wait for the guys in the lab to defrost the little guys. Do you need to empty your bladder?" The nurse paused outside the women's room door. She didn't just look like Helen Reddy, she shared her accent. I nodded. "Meet me in Exam Room 2 when you're done, okay?"

So far, it didn't seem any different than any other appointment with a gynecologist. I ended up in the same procedure room that I'd been in for my first visit, bearing an exam table fitted with stirrups. A paper sheet sat neatly folded on the table. There was a small dressing area off to the side, concealed by a curtain, where I stripped to the waist and draped myself in the sheet, as if it were a floor-length wrap-around skirt.

I sat on the edge of the exam table and waited for Helen to return, wishing I'd thought to bring a sweater. I felt chilled, like I'd been outside in the rain for hours and only a hot bath could warm me. I laid John Barth on the chair next to me, where, I imagined, some other woman's partner might sit. On the wall was a large diagram of the female reproductive cycle and an Anne Geddes' calendar. This month's poster child was a newborn sitting in a bowl filled with small white marbles or pearls. I wondered what kind of mother would sign a newborn up for a photo shoot.

There was a knock on the door. I smoothed the sheet at my waist. My hands were turning blue.

"Well, say hello to these little guys!" Helen said, holding up a vial no bigger than my index finger, full of some pretty pink liquid. It looked like a drink in a shot glass. "Here's your name," she said, pointing to the label on the vial, "here's the donor number. That look right?"

"Yup."

"And here's the post-thaw motility." She showed me a number that meant virtually nothing to me, except I know it was higher than the cutoff for getting your money back from the bank for a poor quality sample. "Ready to get started?"

I nodded and lay back on the table while Helen put on her gloves. I watched her draw up the pink liquid with a thin syringe. It reminded me of the beak of a hummingbird, pollinating flowers in a nature video.

"Scootch toward me," she said when she sat down.

I did.

"More. Put your bottom on the edge of the table." I looked at the pockmarked ceiling, instead of peering at Helen from over my knees. The whole experience was unnervingly intimate. "That's it," she said. "Now relax your legs."

I let my knees fall open. I thought about Dr. Boy, who was probably reading a book in a coffee shop, his cell phone flashing the time next to a stack of books of American cultural criticism and the latest issues of *The New Yorker.* In my mind, he glanced at the time on his phone and checked his messages. He poured creamer into his coffee and sipped it, looking into the distance, before cracking his books. Back in graduate school, even before I first felt the pull of his body, we'd frequented the same coffee shops, studying for our exams and grading student papers. He lived close enough to the clinic that if I called him, he could have been there in twenty minutes, sitting with me and holding my hand.

No. I made the choice to do this alone. I picked up John Barth and held him to my belly.

Helen was fiddling with the light, a paper towel between her gloved hand and the equipment. She tossed the towel in the trash. "You ready?"

I tried to speak but no sound came out.

"Okay. Here goes. First you'll feel me touching you, then you'll feel the speculum. Then I put this tiny little catheter into your cervix. Okay so far?"

I nodded. I felt her warmed gloved hand and the cool speculum. I stared at the marks on the ceiling, counting the small, black indentations. On its way in, the catheter bumped into soft places I didn't know I had. I tried not to wince.

"Now," she said, "I'm going to begin the insemination." I knew if I was going to panic, if I was going to back down and decide to go back to my ordinary life, grading papers and not-dating Dr. Boy, the time was now. It was like the moment the priest says to speak now or forever hold your peace during a wedding ceremony. I took a deep breath, thinking about the first time I'd had sex, back in my college dorm room, after eating take-out Chinese. According to the boy, he'd purchased the condom for twenty-five cents from the vending machine in the men's room down the hall. The women's theoretically sold tampons, but they were always out. In those days, I couldn't think of anything worse than getting pregnant and not finishing school, not graduating summa cum laude with my picture hanging in the student union, and then heading off to graduate school.

All that seemed small and faraway now.

I came back to the room, back to the bright light and Helen's hand on my knee. I imagined the pink liquid in the syringe shooting into the open cavity of my uterus and moving outward, like a bag of minnows dropped into a gallon tank.

"That's it," she said.

"That's it?" The whole procedure took less time than a routine pelvic exam.

"Ready for your Six Flags ride?" She was chipper. I guessed this was probably the highlight of her day, much more interesting than drawing blood or returning phone calls to give the results of negative pregnancy tests.

"Huh?"

She pushed some buttons and raised the end of the table with my legs, until I was nearly upside down, my legs still wrapped in the paper sheet. "Lie here for fifteen to twenty minutes, okay? Gravity helps. Here's your check out form. Just take it to the receptionist when you're done. Here's a list of things you can't do—no hot baths or heavy exercise for twenty-four hours, all common sense stuff. You can take Tylenol but not aspirin if you're feeling crampy. Here's a test requisition; have your progesterone tested in seven days. You can do it at a lab closer to home and have the results sent here for Dr. Williams to review. After fourteen days you can do a home pregnancy test; if it's positive, come in for a blood test." She set the stack of papers on the counter closest to the door. "Any questions?"

"No," I said. "I think I'm good. Thanks."

She smiled. She took my purple file with her. The door clicked shut on her way out.

When she was gone, when I was alone in the room with the vial in the trash and some freshly defrosted sperm working their way up my uterus, I opened John Barth and began to read, imagining those swimmers heading in the direction they were supposed to go. If everything went as planned, they would meet up with an egg in my fallopian tube sometime in the next twelve hours. It didn't seem like such a terribly difficult thing, after all.

After twenty minutes, I got dressed and gathered up my things. At the front desk, I gave the receptionist my credit card, got my parking ticket validated, and headed back toward the highway, everything changed or not changed all at once.

I think most people who haven't done fertility treatment assume insemination involves an actual turkey baster, not a syringe and a catheter not much bigger than a thread. Or that it's some incredibly complicated medical procedure requiring hospitalization. It is what it is, its goal not much different from sex, just without the kissing and fancy lingerie or any of the exertion. I could have done it at home, in the comfort of my own bed, but with less assurance of it working.

On the way home, past the elephant fountain and the elementary school, I parked my car in the lot across from the mall with valet parking. I sniffed my way to the Baby Gap. I fingered the pink onesies and cardigans, dresses rich with spring flowers, jeans the length of my forearm. A woman carrying a baby in a cow-patterned sling rocked back and forth, looking through the clearance items. Another woman bent down and picked up a plush toy her toddler had thrown on the floor. I smiled, conspiratorially. On the rack against the back wall I found a purple bodysuit with a large flower appliquéd on the front. I thought, if I have a boy, this will go to waste. I thought, if I have a newborn in February, she will never be able to wear this (eventually, I learned, winter did come to

Texas). Still, I pulled a size 0-3 months from the rack, with a hat to match. I found two pairs of socks, one purple, one white, and I brought my loot up to the front desk. I already had a stack of onesies stashed in my dresser drawer, next to a package of condoms that had probably long passed their expiration date. Some nights, when I was lonely, I took the clothes from the drawer and spread them on the bed, trying to call up the child who might wear them. Then I refolded them, placing them in order of size, and put them back in the drawer for another day.

"Do you need a gift box and receipt?" the sales girl asked.

"No," I said, "it's for my daughter."

And she looked at me quizzically, as if I couldn't possibly have a daughter. There was no wedding ring on my finger. No newborn in a stroller and an abdomen flat as a young girl's. I took the bag home. I thought, not for the first time, this time next year I could have a three month old. The world seemed full of possibility. And somewhere in the vicinity of my left ovary, I felt something magical open and release.

The week of the insemination, I had sex with Dr. Boy for the first time in almost a year. We'd gone out to dinner at my favorite restaurant in town, watched some stupid Owen Wilson movie while sitting entwined on my couch, and he'd started undressing me before the ending credits rolled.

The whole encounter was fast and heated, something like jealousy hot in his eyes as he moved on top of me. My cervix cramped, and the buzz of impending migraine settled in my left temple. I wasn't sure what the rest of me thought about this latest turn in our ongoing soap opera.

"So how much are you paying to do this?" he said when it was over, pulling on his boxer shorts.

"Well, insurance pays for what they deem legitimate medical expenses, like sonograms. But—oh, you'll like this—they won't pay for, and I quote, 'non-coital reproductive technologies.'

And my insurance only covers IVF for married women who are using their husband's sperm."

"Welcome to Texas. So what do they charge you for it?"

"The cryobank? About $250 for a vial."

He chortled. "Seems like I went into the wrong business. I should sell my services to those in need."

I made a face. I never knew how to take his jokes.

He sat back down on the bed, his hand drawing lazy circles on my belly.

"So you're going to be a mom." His voice glinted with stars.

"Assuming this works, yeah. I mean, I assume it will take a while. Average for a woman my age not doing fertility treatment is six months."

He rubbed his nose and put his glasses back on. I could see him turning something over in his mind, examining it like a ring at the jewelry store. "You know," he said, tucking a strand of hair behind my ear, "you never really asked me what I thought about all this."

I raised my eyebrow, a trick I'd practiced nightly in front of my mirror in high school. "You made it pretty clear that you didn't want to have any part in it."

"I don't. I mean, I like kids. I imagine I'll have some someday. But not now. I'd rather be at the bar having a drink than home changing a diaper."

"And I'd rather be at home."

"But it just seems weird, you doing it this way."

I shrugged. "Feels right to me."

I thought, if this were a made-for-TV movie, there would be a dramatic pause and commercial right here, if this were a made-for-TV movie on Lifetime Television for Women, Dr. Boy would take me in his arms, he would decide to go with me to my next doctor's appointment, he would get involved, he would get so caught up in it that eventually he'd say yes, I want this, I want to be a part of whatever life you are creating with this child, yes, I want to be her father, yes I want to be your spouse, and we would buy a duplex between each of our jobs and we would trade childcare and hours writing, and there would be a happy ending.

Instead, I put on my bathrobe and followed him to the door. He kissed me on the forehead and walked out. I closed the door behind him, wishing I didn't want him in my life, wishing he didn't make me doubt myself.

A few days later, I started bleeding. I didn't know what made me sadder.

7.

THE SUMMER PASSED in a haze of fried chicken and progesterone. After the first attempt, when I started bleeding eight days after the insemination instead of two weeks, Dr. C put me on hormone supplements so my uterine lining stayed in place long enough for an embryo to implant. Melon-colored globes of synthetic progesterone I took with my orange juice in the morning and when I brushed my teeth at night. She also prescribed progesterone suppositories, which I special-ordered from the compounding pharmacy in town. I kept them in my fridge, next to the stick of margarine, to keep them cool; they looked like little white bullets encased in their plastic packaging. I broke down the word as I ripped the package at the dotted line—pro-gest-er-one—that which promoted gestation.

I took them for half of each month, starting the day after the insemination. They controlled the luteal phase of my menstrual cycle. They made me hungry and sleepy. I ate fried chicken and potato salad and tuna melts until I gained five pounds and didn't fit into any of my clothes. I spent my days trying to write or walking around a local park. In the evenings I watched TV and went to sleep early.

Dr. Boy sublet a friend's Greenwich Village apartment, and I had the summer to myself. I was alone. My body was my only companion.

The experience was intoxicating, like Sunday afternoons drinking merlot and wandering around campus my first year in graduate school. I have never before or since been so obsessed with the state of my lower abdomen. I stockpiled ovulation prediction kits and home pregnancy tests. I charted the color and consistency of my cervical fluid, every twinge, cramp, headache. The vague metallic taste in my mouth. I wrote the notes on graph paper and kept them in the drawer of my bedside table, along with the expired condoms and the baby clothes I hoped to use next year. I felt cells divide and multiply, the loveliest mathematics. The world seemed slightly off balance; I felt like I was walking on textured carpet in high-heeled sandals. I slowed down, my steps cautious and deliberate.

I began to imagine the child I'd have the end of February, the end of March, the end of April. For two weeks of every month—the two weeks between the trip down the highway for the date with the frozen vial and the pregnancy test fourteen days later—I was pregnant and not pregnant all at once. I told myself my daughter would arrive as winter turned to spring; I would take the summer and learn the inches of her new skin, the location of her freckles and the creases in her thighs. I would learn myself through her.

Beneath the progesterone fog lay a pulsing urgency I couldn't control. I wanted to be pregnant now. So in August, after three failed cycles, I conceded to my doctor's professional opinion and filled my prescription for Clomid, a drug commonly used to promote ovulation. She had me on the lowest possible dose; I halved the round white pills on my kitchen counter and chased them with decaffeinated green tea. I'd given up caffeine, alcohol, and my favorite migraine medication. I walked miles around the track at the park, watching pint-sized soccer players run in the field and thinking about pushing my daughter in a stroller. I went to bed at 10:00 every night. I went to yoga class and stretched, then worried about unmooring something that shouldn't be unmoored, so I gave up abdominal exercises of all kinds. My belly softened. I folded up a sweater and put it under my T-shirt when I walked around my apartment.

Sometimes I fell asleep that way, with my hand on the swell of a fake pregnancy.

On the third day of my fourth treatment cycle, I drove to the clinic. It was a Saturday, a day when there wasn't much traffic on the road between here and there, when the university was largely abandoned and they didn't have valet parking out front. I parked in the back lot, and followed barely navigable directions Helen had dictated over the phone, down corridors and up elevators and across skyways until I landed at the back door of the clinic, with the drop box for the lab outside. I felt like a child following a treasure map, like something out of the 1980s film *Goonies*. And then I weaved down the familiar hall until I found myself next to wannabe pregnant women and their husbands and the token lesbian couple.

I took a deep breath and sat in the row of chairs outside the nurses' station. I took out my book and tried to read. A nurse I'd never met before, with a bob of silver hair, called women back to the sonogram room one by one. Finally it was my turn; she ushered me in, gave me a paper gown to cover my legs, and let me wait for the doctor.

Inside the sonogram room was a door to a small bathroom where, I gathered, I was supposed to strip to the waist and cover myself with a sheet. The routine was all too familiar. On the back of the toilet was a small basket filled with sanitary pads and tampons.

I hoped I didn't bleed too much while I sat waiting. It hadn't really occurred to me until the drive here that a day 3 sonogram inevitably meant a sonogram during my period.

On the wall hung the familiar diagram of the female reproductive cycle and a picture of in vitro fertilization, all the sperm crowning around and one lucky cell penetrating the egg. To my right, on a cart beside the exam table was a computer monitor and a printer and a bin full of medical supplies. To my left, there was another monitor.

The doctor, one of the interns in reproductive endocrinology, knocked on the door and came in. I smoothed the paper sheet. He introduced himself, and I promptly forgot his real name. I was too busy watching him prepare for the sonogram, holding up a phallic-shaped transducer and slapping a condom on it with a familiar latex thwack.

This was going to be a transvaginal sonogram, to get a look at my ovaries and the lining of my uterus.

I thought about the oversized dildo a friend had been given as a gag gift in college. I'm sure my mouth dropped open in astonishment. I supposed he'd done the procedure so many times that he'd forgotten how funny it was, though I supposed finding it funny would have broken professional etiquette. I wondered if he and the other doctors laughed about it over coffee.

As I stared at this condom-covered, penis-shaped thing, he said, "It looks pretty big, doesn't it?"

My eyes widened.

"Don't worry," Dr. Probe said seriously, "the whole thing doesn't go in."

I tried not to snort.

Starting that night, I took my half tablet of Clomid for five days in order to stimulate the follicles to grow. I waited for side effects, but other than the bright flashes of migraine aura the first day, I felt nothing but the headiness of estrogen and then an indescribable itching in the area I assumed my ovaries were. They felt like they were taking up too much space. They felt like they were going to burst. I understood why when I went back for my repeat sonogram on day 9 and the doctor pointed out two grape-sized circles (the follicles that held mature eggs) and numerous smaller ones. Exactly what the doctor wanted to see. They were beautiful, round as Challah on Rosh Hashanah. And my uterine lining was beautiful; it looked, as the doctor said, like an Oreo cookie, three glorious layers that meant my body was ready to conceive a child.

I was overwhelmed with estrogen and possibility. This time,

when I returned to the clinic a few days later for the insemination, I brought a pair of baby socks a friend had given me
when I told her I wanted to have a child. They were pink. I
was pink. The world around me tinted rose. Even the nurse
said I looked radiant.

Joanna's hands moved over my body in the massage room. She
worked from hip to toe and shoulder to fingertip, outward,
pulling tension from my body. I wondered how she released
it from her own.

"I need to tell you," I think I said as her hands moved toward
my ankle. "There's a chance I could be pregnant, I mean, I'm
trying to get pregnant. I know there are places I shouldn't be
touched?" There was a spot—I didn't know where exactly—
that if you pushed on it hard enough, it stimulated uterine
contractions, miscarriage or labor.

"That's here," she said, touching lightly. "And there's another
here." She placed her thumb against a soft pad in my hand.

I think she must have asked me if I had a partner. And as her
hands worked over my body our stories unfolded and wove
together. I was a single woman trying to have a baby and she
was a thrice-married woman who had lost several children.
Childlessness was thick in the room.

"I made peace with it," she said. "I understand now the path
my life has taken. I have two stepdaughters I adore. I have
helped them grow into beautiful young women." Her hands
moved back up, and she worked at a stubborn spot beneath
my shoulder blade. "But it took me a long time to get here."

I got dressed and left, and I felt my body open. I watched
people walking downtown, going to lunch or to the bank or
the new antique stores and boutiques of women's clothes.
This was my home now, the ramshackle downtown that was
slowly becoming gentrified, this town without a real bookstore
or library to call its own. But it had Joanna and the women
who came to take her yoga class. An hour down the highway

was Dr. Williams' office and the Whole Foods and the café I sat in sometimes, after my appointments at the clinic. And school was about to start again. I was sure everyone could see the baby in my eyes. I was heavier and lighter all at once and never quite really there. I was always driving to the clinic or thinking about the clinic or the vague twinges in the pit of my abdomen. I wondered how I would ever be able to concentrate long enough to read a novel or grade a stack of papers, with all those hormones thrumming my veins.

I couldn't sit still. I went to campus and checked my mail and wandered through the union, watching the new students escort their parents to the bookstore for College T-shirts and sweat suits. Outside the cafeteria, I saw another faculty member with her new baby in a stroller. She worked in another division so I didn't know her well, but something in me broke open, and I looked at her with longing.

I was sure, as I had ever been sure of anything, that I was pregnant. When Helen had called me to give me the results of my progesterone test a few days ago, the number was sky high, over one hundred. On my first cycle, it had been a pathetic seven. "That's a great number," she'd said, and I could hear the astonishment in her voice, "keep your fingers crossed!"

I sat down beside Janine on the bench, next to a stained Winnie the Pooh blanket, a cloth-covered rattle, a bottle with the cap off. I looked at the baby, with a shock of dark hair and vaguely crossed eyes, dressed in a yellow onesie stained with spit up.

"Wow. She's adorable," I said. I never knew what to say to new mothers, whether they wanted to talk about their babies or talk about anything but their babies. Someday, I thought, I would know the secret mommy handshake and be able to share anecdotes about the trials of parenting at dinner parties.

"Would you like to feed her?" Janine said.

"Sure." I took the baby in my arms and felt the heavy weight of her head settle next to my breast. I put the bottle in her mouth and watched her swallow. She sputtered and coughed. A year ago, I held Max on Aimee's couch, breastmilk soaking my T-shirt. That was the last time I'd held a baby.

"Hold her up a little bit," Janine coaxed. Her voice was soft, without judgment.

I sat the baby higher, and she continued sucking. Some day I would know how to do this, some day I would know all the things you need to know to be a mother, which car seat to buy and how to open a stroller with one hand, and how to get a baby to drink from a bottle.

"That looks good on you," I think is what Karen said when she saw us. Karen was the senior colleague who served as unofficial mentor for most of the young women faculty, and the baby's self-proclaimed grandmother. She had an infant seat in her car to tote the baby around town and I saw her often pushing a stroller on campus. The three of us sat together for a while, just looking at the sucking baby.

Then Janine took her back and carried her across the hall to the bathroom where, I presumed, she would change the baby's diaper. She had taken a large tote bag with her; it bulged with baby wipes and cloth diapers and extra onesies.

"Do you have something to tell me?" Karen asked when we were alone.

I thought, she knows, she knows. She can see it in the new roundness of my face, the five pounds of soul food. She knows, and she wants me to confide in her. Exactly a year ago, Janine had "something to tell" Karen, a something that now weighed roughly fifteen pounds.

I didn't really know what I was doing there, on campus on a Saturday morning when all the students were arriving with their SUVs full of televisions and laptop computers and clothes. Ordinarily, I'd want to be anyplace but here. I just couldn't be at home anymore. Caught, I asked Karen a question about the new class I was going to teach, a class on representations of the family. We would watch episodes of *Full House* and *Leave it to Beaver* and talk about how the family had changed in American culture. I asked whatever question I made up on the spur of the moment, and the threat of discovery vanished. I took my pregnant or not-pregnant self home, more optimistic than I'd been in a long time. My second year in Texas was starting, and though I knew it was not my permanent home, I felt welcome by the trees that lined campus, by colleagues walking with cups of coffee and stacks of books balanced in their hands, by the possibility of new friends and students. I wondered, when I did get pregnant, how I would tell them.

8.

THE WOMAN WHO WANTS TO BE PREGNANT stands in the bathroom holding the First Response test up to the light. Negative is blank. This one isn't blank. But it isn't shockingly pink. There's a line, the palest pink line, a baby pink line, and in the line is possibility and hope. She wants so badly to believe. She goes to the lab and gets a blood test. The phlebotomist snaps on the tourniquet; she rolls the dark tubes in her hand. The woman notes every cramp. Her uterus sits heavy in her pelvis. Her friends on the Internet tell her that any line is a positive result and she wants to believe. Only her uterus knows the truth, and as she leaves the clinic it reveals itself in a rush of blood.

Sitting here now, I remember in the pit of my stomach, in the clenched fist between my shoulder blades, in the thrum of migraine welling behind my eyes, what it felt like living in a body that wasn't yet pregnant but wanted to be. I hold in my shoulders long hours of driving back and forth to the city, hands clenched on the wheel, pop tunes on the radio. The Year of Madonna, the Year of Erasure, the Year of Sheryl Crow. All those mornings I spent driving between here and there, drafting poems and planning lessons as the miles ticked past on the odometer. All those nights I was so tired from hormone supplements that all I could do was curl up on the couch and watch TV.

The woman who wants to be pregnant takes another pregnancy test, holds it up to the light. I want to tell her to throw the stick in the trash, to drink margaritas with a friend, to cancel her appointment at the clinic. I want to tell the woman who wants to be pregnant that it will turn out okay. That there is a baby, her baby, waiting wrapped in an embroidered blanket, with arms outstretched. I want her to tell her that she will know the feeling of feet tickling the walls of her womb. I want her to know that she will go full term. She will deliver a child. And they will thrive together. But if I tried to tell her that, she wouldn't listen. She would say, how do you know? How do you know that I'm not infertile, just like the papers from the clinic say? And she would be right.

The woman who wants to be pregnant sits on the bathroom floor. She turns the test stick in her hands, studies it like a work of art, noting its streaky blues. She missed her friend's wedding for this. Lee, in a white dress, marrying a Native American painter she met at an artist colony. She missed her dear friend's wedding for the chance of having a baby in May. A baby in June, she thinks, a baby in July. What is she willing to give up for the slightest possibility of a child? Her best friends aren't speaking to her anymore. Some days, she's not sure that she cares.

The woman who wants to be pregnant throws the stick in the trash. In the mirror she sees herself age. She is no longer a girl. She fingers the deep-set lines around her eyes, rubs lotion into chapped hands. There is a single strand of white in her dark hair; she pulls it out by the root, throws it into the garbage. It coils serpentine on used Kleenex, spent test sticks, sanitary pads.

Go to the wedding, I want to say; go on vacation with your family; live your life. But I can't tell her to trade the possibility of a child for a party or anything else. She has only one chance each month, twelve chances in a year, to become a mother. She has better odds, she's sure, of getting in a car accident on the way to the clinic. It needs to be her choice, and every day she will wake up, take her vitamins, drink decaffeinated tea, and choose the baby. She will risk losing her friends. They write her notes, saying they don't understand her anymore, saying she is obsessed. Her days orbit around her pelvis.

In a file folder, in a drawer in her nightstand, she keeps the checkout forms from the clinic. Every month, in small black letters, she reads insurance code 628.9: infertility, female, unknown.

Thursday, September 12: Drove to the clinic for monitoring before afternoon class. While waiting, read articles about reproductive technologies for family class, which is quite surreal. Getting discouraged. Will try this month and next and then take a break until summer. Too hard to travel back and forth with teaching schedule.

Friday, September 13: Drove to the clinic for monitoring. Still nothing much going on.

Saturday, September 14: Drove to the clinic for monitoring: finally (!!!), one follicle close to mature (16 mm), several others midsize (11 mm or so). Will go back on Monday for last sono and will probably trigger with HCG shot (for IUI on Tues/Wed). Stopped at bookstore on the way home to grade. Read a book on fertility diets and blood type. Seems sort of silly, but I'll try anything.

Sunday, September 15: Positive OPK, which means I need to schedule an IUI for tomorrow. Left a message with the on call doc; he said to keep my afternoon appointment, which is good, because I teach all morning. If I leave at noon, I can be there around 1:30. This really is getting insane.

Monday, September 16: Well, this takes the cake. I was standing in class today, talking to my fresh(wo)men about something, and I felt that tell-tale ping of ovulation on my left side. Two hours later I was lying on a table for a sonogram which revealed that I still hadn't ovulated but, in fact, my follicle was on the small side of ripe (19 mm). The sonogram doc called my RE who said I should take an OPK right then and if it was positive, I'd do my second IUI in the morning and if it was negative, to take the HCG shot and then come in on Weds. for IUI #2. Of course it was negative because I'd been drinking water all day and my urine was diluted! The nurse thought the same thing so she drew my blood, and I had an IUI while my blood went to the lab to be tested for LH. By the time I got home the nurse had left me a message saying that I had clearly surged and to come back in for my second IUI in the am, and not—very adamantly!!—to do the shot.

Tuesday, September 17: I have driven to Big City five times in the last six days. Drove to the clinic for second IUI this cycle, then home for afternoon class.

Wednesday, September 18: Bloated.

Thursday, September 19: Really woozy—possible side effect of Prometrium?

Wednesday, September 25: So tired. All I want to do is curl up in bed with Pistachio and a movie on the laptop.

Wednesday, October 2: Hit 16 DPO and still no spotting. No positive pregnancy test either. Oh-kay.

Thursday, October 3: Went to see Consuelo for a blood pregnancy test. Started bleeding the minute I left the clinic. On to cycle #6.

9.

THE EMAIL SAID that the women met on the last Sunday of the month to share information and anecdotes about being single mothers. They met in the Big City, so close to the airport that I could watch planes descend as I parked my car in the lot. I sat in my car a long time, surveying the other vehicles, the minivans and SUVs. A woman with curly brown hair pulled a stroller out of her trunk, popped it open with one hand, and then snapped an infant seat in with the other; it was one of those things called a "travel system" that Aimee had told me about when she was pregnant with Max. Her other child, a girl with straight black hair, must have been six or seven, sporting a pink Dora the Explorer backpack over a pink T-shirt. She skipped beside her mother, her face turned toward the sun. The woman stopped by the door and spoke into the intercom; she was buzzed into the building.

After the next minivan came into the parking lot, I grabbed my backpack and my plastic container full of oatmeal cookies and made my way up to the intercom. The meeting was held at a large conference room at one of the moms' office buildings.

I signed in at the desk and followed the noise of children playing. There were four tables pushed together, like the seminar room where I taught. I put the cookies on the table reserved for food and stared at the offerings, store bought sugar cookies decorated with pink frosting and multicolored sprinkles, an open bag of Doritos, and a bowl full of grapes. I stood in front of the table until a woman offered to pour me a cup of apple juice.

"Thanks," I said. That's when I realized I was unquestionably the youngest person in the room.

"Are you the babysitter?" she asked. "The kids are in the next room over."

"No," I said, using my best Texas smile. "This is my first meeting. I'm Robin."

"Sorry for the assumption. You just look so young! I'm Marisol." She gestured toward the small boy holding her leg. "This is Miguel. He's two and a half."

"He's cute."

"You make these cookies? They look great."

"Yeah. Gave me something to do last night."

"That won't be a problem when you have one of these!" She ruffled Miguel's hair and smiled down at him. "I'm going to see if I can get him to stay with the other kids. Good to meet you." She picked Miguel up and tickled his belly. "Let's go, you," she said to the little boy. "Let's go see your friends!"

I watched her leave, Miguel riding high on her shoulder. I sat down at one of the tables with my cup of juice and a cookie. One by one the women filed in, and I listened to them talk about soccer practice and power struggles about homework. A couple of them were obviously pregnant, wearing shapeless maternity tops and jeans. One had a baby tucked under her shirt, nursing him to sleep.

We went around the table introducing ourselves, munching on grapes. I could hear the kids yelling in the next room.

It felt like the first day of school. My palms were sweaty and my hair was falling out of my ponytail and there were a couple grease stains, I noticed, on my white T-shirt. "I'm Robin," I said. "I'm a professor of English," I added, in case anyone doubted I was old enough to be there. The group didn't have any official minimum age, but with few exceptions, it seemed like everyone else was at least thirty-five before they started considering having kids on their own. They called it "Plan B." They came to single motherhood after failed relationships and waiting around for Mr. Right until all they could hear was the shrieking alarm of their biological clocks. Some of them waited so long they needed egg donors or surrogates or gave up and adopted. Their stories depressed me; I wasn't the kind of person who would sit around and wait for something I wanted. "I've been trying for five months and I'm getting really impatient."

They bombarded me with advice. "Which doctor are you working with? You should try the Pappas'. They're the best group in town. Best thing I ever did was switch docs."

"You should take baby aspirin," one of the women said.

"Have you had an HSG yet?"

"Are you doing one IUI per cycle or two?"

"Get a new donor. After five cycles, it's definitely time to move on."

I wrote down their questions in my notebook. I had a lot of things to ask Helen at my next appointment.

"Did you use a new donor?" Mary asked. Mary was the nurse who always prayed before she did the insemination.

"Yeah, why?" I leaned back on my elbows, watching her draw the specimen into the syringe.

"His stats look great. I don't think I've ever seen numbers like this."

"Cool." Donor number two didn't have a Ph.D., but he was a philosophy major, so I decided he'd made peace with whatever existential angst he might have had about donating his sperm. His favorite animal was a dog, but I wouldn't hold that against him. At least he had green eyes. After the meeting with other single moms, I called the cryobank and ordered three vials to be shipped to my doctor's office on dry ice.

Mary settled herself between my legs. "Please, God, bless us with a child."

I held the pair of pink baby socks in my hands like a talisman.

Please, I thought, please. I willed myself pregnant.

"The timing is good," Mary said, swabbing my cervix clean. She held the swab to show me. "You are ready to conceive a child."

It took Mary a long time to find the opening. It hurt. I would probably bleed.

"I am inseminating you now," she said, her voice big and prophetic.

I the corner of my right eye I saw a crown of light. It flickered and sparked, like a crystal held up in the sunlight.

Mary touched my belly on her way out of the room. My skin burned under her hand.

I closed my eyes and breathed. I exhaled slowly, releasing the day. It was all so surreal. Just two hours ago I was standing in front of my class, prattling on about new forms of American families. Families formed by adoption, by the joining of two divorced parents, by lesbian moms. We talked about chosen families, instead of biological ones. I could see the resistance in their eyes. These were girls from small towns who married at nineteen, even if they called themselves feminists.

It was almost midterm, the point in the semester when I began to coast, doing what needed to be done to reach the end and start all over again the next term. When class ended, I made a note on my calendar that I needed to schedule appointments with all my student advisees, who needed to pick their spring classes. I gathered up my things started heading to the student union for a drink, thinking about what I was going to do with my afternoon. Comment on the never-ending stack of student papers or read the novel for my advanced literature course. It wasn't until I poured myself a cup of apple juice and popped the plastic lid on the cup that I remembered I needed to be at the clinic. I rushed to the car. I made it down the highway in record time.

"You'll never believe what happened," I told Mary when she ushered me into the exam room. "I was supposed to do my trigger shot at midnight on Saturday, and the lights went out! I live in the country, and it was pitch black. I thought I'd have to give myself a shot in the dark!" I'd laughed about the pun all weekend; getting pregnant was a long shot, a shot in the dark. I kept myself awake with the blue light reflecting off the screen of my laptop; if I had a flashlight, I couldn't find it. The lights went back on at 11:30; I drew up the diluent and mixed it with the powder. I drew the medicine into the syringe, swapped the thick needle for the slim intramuscular one, rubbed alcohol on my left thigh, and jabbed myself with the needle. The medication burned going in. I slept the deep sleep of a pregnant woman and woke nauseated and headachey. It was the cruelest irony of fertility treatment; the drug used to induce ovulation mimicked early pregnancy symptoms.

The story was funnier in my head.

I checked the time on my watch. I'd been lying there for the requisite fifteen minutes. Time to go.

I found Mary in the nurse's station on my way out. I remembered I had a tin full of oatmeal cookies for her and the other staff to share stashed in my backpack. I'd baked them on Sunday, in a fit of post-HCG-shot nesting, before meeting my friend Nona for coffee. I traded her the cookies for my check out papers.

It was cold outside, turning to fall. I drove home with the spark of light in the corner of my eye, and it was still there when I picked up Nona to go to dinner at Karen's. My uterus cramped and stretched. I tried to ignore it.

"How'd it go?" Nona asked as she slid into the passenger seat of my car. She was one of two people in town who knew about the Baby Plan. Last week, on our way to an art festival, she'd gone with me to my day 3 sonogram. She sat and graded papers in the waiting area while Dr. Probe got a good look at my ovaries.

I shrugged. "Ask me in two weeks."

In the few months since Nona had joined the department,

she became my co-conspirator, like Aimee or Lee, driving down the highway with eighties mix tapes on the car stereo. We talked about students. We talked about our siblings. We talked about her boyfriend and Dr. Boy. We shared Indian food and Thai food and Mexican food. We sat next to each other at faculty meetings, and we drove to the Big City. I helped her paint the rooms of her house, both of us dressed in flannel shirts and ponytails.

Tonight she was in jeans and a flowing jade shirt; turquoise dangled from her ears. "So, any ideas what this dinner is about?"

"No clue." Last week, we'd received a summons from Karen, printed on College stationery, that she wanted to have us for dinner.

"What do you think her story is?" It was one of our favorite games, speculating on the private lives of the older female faculty. We made up elaborate fantasies where they had lesbian lovers in other departments, they lost fiancés during the Vietnam War, they had affairs with men at Big City University. There wasn't much to do in the Middle of Nowhere, North Texas, other than hang out in the Wal-Mart parking lot, and there was nothing but reruns on TV. We needed our own soap opera.

The truth was, I thought, that I was the one with the big secret. I felt like Clark Kent sometimes, hiding my superhero identity and dashing into phone booths to change. The only difference was I wore a paper sheet instead of a cape, and the only world I was trying to save was my own.

I had to admit it was nice, going to dinner and having normal things to do instead of going home to think about some sperm swimming through my uterus and not having sex with Dr. Boy.

I drank a glass of white wine and forgot about my ovaries and settled into the cozy warmth of Karen's home. I pet her dogs. I looked at the African art on the walls, the pictures of nieces and nephews. I wondered, if thirty years ago, Karen had been like me, coveting other people's children. There was no future tonight; there was only now, a glass full of wine, a warm bowl of stew, and a spent vial in the clinic trashcan.

It was October. I thought about autumn in Indiana, the piles of leaves on the long walk to campus. I thought about flannel lined jackets and hand-knit sweaters, mugs of hot chocolate or Lady Grey tea. It would have been easy to get swallowed up in sorrow. I decided not to revel in sadness but seek out companionship in quiet patches of sunlight. I sat with Nona on her porch, watching the neighbor kids ride their bikes until the sun went down.

I had trouble staying in one place. Even when I didn't need to be at the clinic I found myself on the highway, holing up in a coffee shop or bookstore on the outskirts of the city. I drove to visit other single moms. I drove to the lake campus and sat and imagined myself somewhere else.

Twelve days after the insemination—cycle day twenty-four—I sat at the coffee shop halfway between here and there, drinking coffee because there was no reason not to drink coffee. I ate a bagel and cream cheese that tasted like soap, punishment because I shouldn't have been eating it anyway. Dairy products made me ill. I went across the street to Old Navy and bought a pair of jeans one size bigger than I usually wore because my waistline was expanding by the minute, mocking me with pounds rather than pregnancy. And when I got home, I found that my period had started two days early. I put on a pantiliner and kicked the garbage can.

I had an appointment to see the Dr. C in two weeks, to talk about the next phase. I knew she would want to talk about heavy-duty drugs, the shots patients called injectables, or maybe even in vitro fertilization. At the end of the month I would be thirty, self-imposed baby deadline, and still childless. I felt hollow. I imagined the unimaginable: that years down the road I would still be driving down that highway, having my ovaries looked at, with no baby to show for it. I was, as everyone kept telling me, young. I didn't have just a handful of eggs tucked in a back corner of my ovary, a year away from menopause. Theoretically, I could spend more than ten years on this baby project. The thought was terrifying.

I thought about the bagel. I thought about the cramping in my lower abdomen I'd first noticed during my students' midterm on Friday. I thought about the heart palpitations that started a few days ago, and the funny taste in my mouth. I thought about the bleeding, just some half moons in my underwear. I sent a quick email to a friend who told me to take a pregnancy test. I was all out. I drove to Walgreens, one hand on my belly.

I didn't need to read the directions. I unwrapped the package. I peed. And by the time I set the stick on the counter I was staring at two blue lines, clear and easy as the name foretold.

All I could do was laugh. I took out my graph paper and wrote in big letters next to the day's date, PREGNANT (3w5d).

Part III

1.

THE REST OF THE WEEKEND passed in a haze of pink onesies and disbelief. In some soft pocket of my uterus a child was growing: a child so small his heart wasn't yet beating, he didn't have arms or legs or even a discernible sex, but he had the power to make me sleep, to retch at the faintest of smells, to change everything I believed about the world. I was going to be a mother come July.

Monday morning before my first class, I drove to the lab for blood pregnancy test. Consuelo, the dark-haired phlebotomist who had snapped a tourniquet around my bicep at least once a month for the past six months, asked, as she always did, if I'd had something to eat. She put a label bearing my name on the tube, rolled it in her hand like a talisman. The needle slid into my vein. I stared at the sharps box on the wall, thinking everything you need to know about me is here, in this thick red blood. The tube would be picked up and taken to a larger lab, somewhere in the city, for processing, and the results would be faxed to my doctor, across town. Helen or Mary would jot it down in my file, call Dr. C. A solid beta HCG level was the first of many milestones; at four weeks of pregnancy, I'd learned from reading around on the internet, it averaged 100 units.

I went to class that day a working mom. I felt light, heady with estrogen and progesterone. A sleeve of saltines poked out of my backpack. I sipped from a bottle of water and tried not to pass out during class. While my students answered questions about short stories, I hung on single words like a life preserver. I wondered how I would be able to get anything done. I would be pregnant for the rest of the school year. It seemed unfathomable.

In the afternoon, I stood in my office, arranging the poems of my book manuscript. They lay on the carpet like an archipelago of paper. I printed a cover letter and put it in an envelope. I walked it across campus to the post office. Nona left a basket of apples outside my door, sweet and round as the new year.

When I got home, I took another pregnancy test. The second line was a solid dark purple. I lined them up on the counter, six in all. Pregnant pregnant pregnant. The word was full.

I fell asleep before dusk, the cat nuzzled against my belly purring.

I dreamed about a boy with dark curly hair, this child of a scientist and a poet, the most eloquent chemistry. We went to the park on a warm spring afternoon, picked berries in the woods, made pancakes on Sunday mornings. I dreamed of taking him swimming in orange floaties, with a white hat tied under his chin. And then I dreamed he was washed out to sea, pulled under the high tide.

I woke to a fist clenched in my abdomen and a wave of blood on the sheets. In the bathroom, it dripped and speckled the tile floor. I held a wad of toilet paper between my legs and pulled it away. It was nail polish bright.

I went back to bed, shivering. I dialed Helen's number at the clinic, mumbled the words *positive* and *miscarriage* on her voicemail. It didn't occur to me to go to the E.R. I closed my eyes. Stay, I told the curly-haired boy, I barely know you. Stay.

It wasn't even 8:00 when the phone rang.

"Robin," Helen said softly, "tell me what's going on."

I answered her in another woman's voice. "I don't know. I think I'm having a miscarriage or something. I mean, I had a positive pregnancy test and now I'm bleeding."

"Okay," she said. "I just called the lab to get the results of your beta from yesterday. It's 78. That's a good first number.

Are you still taking the progesterone?"

"Yes."

"Sometimes you can spot from the suppositories."

"This isn't spotting."

"How much blood are we talking about?"

I thought about the stained sheets, the bathroom tile, the wet pad between my legs. "I don't know. It seems like a lot."

"A tablespoon? A cup?"

I thought of my measuring spoons, nested together in a kitchen drawer, the cookies I'd baked for Mary. "I don't know. I don't know."

"Okay." Her voice was calm with an undercurrent of something darker. "Can you drive? I know it's a long drive. Can you come down here so we can check you out?"

"Yes." I didn't have to think about it. I would leave a message for the department secretary and tell her I needed to cancel my classes for the day. That's what any mother would do.

Ford trucks lined up on the highway to Big City, people going to their office jobs, chatting on their cell phones. As I sat in rush hour traffic, fresh blood trickled between my legs.

At the clinic, I sat with the other women who wanted to be pregnant waiting for their sonograms. For me, the hallway was irrevocably changed. I was still bleeding when I lay down on the table and opened my legs, when the doctor I had nicknamed Dr. Pretty inserted the condomed transducer, which didn't seem so funny today.

"Last period?" Dr. Pretty said. I couldn't remember. Only one date seemed important.

"Estimated due date is July 6," Mary said. That was Lee's birthday.

"Now you understand," he said carefully, "that it's much too early to see anything. But any time there's bleeding, we need to check for an ectopic." He pointed out the two burst follicles, the uterine lining that was still thick, pregnancy thick,

Mary said, and yes, the tubes looked clear but I would need to be monitored closely, that they couldn't rule anything out. "These are good signs," Mary said, "I'm glad. You know I told Helen I'm this baby's dad." They took my blood, again, in the lab, to check progesterone, to see if my beta was going up or down. And I drove home, to wait.

Every two days I drove to the clinic to have my blood drawn; every two days I waited for the phone call to come with the results. Other than the day of the bleeding, the number rose, as it was supposed to, with every draw.

I was still pregnant the next week when I went to see Dr. C for the appointment that was supposed to be my gear-up-to-try-the-next-thing pep talk. I wore the same black suit I'd worn when I met her last spring, only now I couldn't button the pants.

"Six months?!" she greeted me, cheerily, eyes wide.

Six months. Six months of the highway, six months of pills, six months of Dr. Pretty and Dr. Probe, six months of weight gain and no baby, six months of living between here and there, pregnant and not pregnant all at once.

She was more beautiful than I remembered her, her hair pulled back in a sleek ponytail. This time she wore a wedding ring. She had a husband. Did she have a child of her own? Did she need fertility drugs? Did she ever lose a baby? I watched her while she thumbed through the pages of my chart. It was as thick as my doctoral dissertation. Its purple cover was the same shade as the onesie I bought after my first IUI. I yawned and sank back into the upholstered chair. The drive had exhausted me. I felt groggy and off balance, like I was taking cold medicine. It was hard to believe I wasn't yet six weeks along. A full pregnancy was forty.

"So," she said. "You did three natural cycles, three cycles with Clomid and HCG trigger. Positive pregnancy test last week. And you changed donors this cycle? Interesting." She continued her review, solving the greatest possible proof. Do you have any questions?"

I didn't know where to start. "Just about the bleeding, I guess."

"The bleeding." A question mark swirled in her green eyes. She looked down at my chart.

"Has it stopped?"

There hadn't been a day yet I hadn't bled. "It's just spotting now."

She nodded. "Some women just bleed during early pregnancy and it doesn't mean anything. Your beta levels have been doubling every two days—that's what we like to see. Progesterone looks fine." She looked at me conspiratorially. "Should we take a peek?"

As Dr. Pretty had done, she warned me that we might not be able to see anything, it was still early, five weeks and two days, my beta level just over 1500, when you can begin to see a gestational sac on a sonogram, and about a week too early to see the heartbeat.

She disappeared somewhere to check on another patient while I sat out in the hall, waiting for the sonogram room to open.

"She doing a sono on you?" Helen asked as she walked by. Her white sneakers squeaked on the floor.

Then she and Dr. C conferred in the doorway to the nurse's station. I wondered what they were talking about, another patient's IVF cycle, or my hormone levels, or the blood that wouldn't stop.

Every other time I'd had a sonogram the nurse brought me into the small room, and I'd go into the adjoining bathroom, wrap a sheet around my waist and then hop on the table, legs clamped together, to wait before the doctor would knock and come in. Today, it was just the two of us—no need for a nurse with a female doc—and she fiddled with the equipment in the outer room while I undressed behind the bathroom door. It struck me as horribly intimate, more intimate than love or even sex. She knew my body better than anyone else in the world.

We were two women who created a child together.

She was slow, tender. She moved the wand between my legs, both of our eyes on the television monitor. I couldn't bear to look at her. "Lining looks good. That spot keeps coming back. See it?" A black circle, small as a child's fingernail, surrounded by a white ring in the center of my uterus. "That's the sac." And somewhere inside it was the speck of a child, in the process of becoming, cell by cell. If I looked hard enough, I could probably see him grow.

"I think," she finally said, wiggling the wand around to see my ovaries, "with the bleeding, you tried to implant two." I never wanted twins, but loss swelled inside me. "I don't see anything where it shouldn't be, but we need to watch this closely. Schedule another sonogram for next week."

I dressed slowly, taking a fresh pad from the basket of linens. In the consult room she used as an office, Dr. C wrote down the names of local obstetricians on the back of her business card. "This is what we should see next week," she said, drawing the sac that we saw today and the small shapeless blob of an embryo and another white balloon, called the yolk, which feeds the embryo during early pregnancy. "And if something goes wrong," she paused, her eyes fixed on my own, "we start over." She said it gently. She never said the words *miscarriage* or *loss*. "We know you can get pregnant now. And that's an amazing thing."

On my way out, she stuffed boxes of progesterone samples in my hands, double my usual dose. "No horseback riding," she teased. "No yoga class. Just take it easy. Go to work and come home from work. Sit or lie down as much as possible. And stop at the lab," she said, checking another box on the test requisition form. "I want to check on your estradiol level too."

I was too tired to be panicked on the way home.

I don't remember most of the drive to the clinic—the hour on the highway—but I remember passing the bank at the corner, turning on to Sparrow and sitting in traffic. The leaves on the trees were starting to turn. It was the middle of November. In a few weeks it would be Thanksgiving, the anniversary of my grandmother's death, and my thirtieth birthday. I looked at all the expensive houses lined up by the university, the elephant fountain in a well-manicured yard, the Baby Gap where I had gone after my first trip to the clinic.

My heart raced with the car's engine. I remembered that black spot on the monitor and I thought, it will be there again today. Since I'd seen Dr. C, I'd been researching early pregnancy loss—chemical pregnancies, ectopic pregnancies, blighted ova.

In the sonogram room, Dr. Pretty waved his magic wand between my legs. He called out to the nurse. "Gestational sac: size five weeks, five days."

I knew without him saying anything. It measured a week too small to be viable.

"Yolk?" the nurse asked.

"No." To me, Dr. Pretty said quite simply, "I'll talk to your doctor. I imagine she will tell you to stop taking progesterone. But she might want to do a D&C."

I think I said, "I want to talk to her." I wouldn't believe it until I heard it from her. She'd said the numbers were doubling properly, everything looked fine.

"She's in surgery right now. I'll see if she can call you later."

They left me alone in the room. My fingers fumbled with the buttons on my pants.

When I saw Helen in the hallway, she handed me a travel-sized box of Kleenex. Just six weeks in, my first pregnancy was over.

(Loss: Interlude)

I THOUGHT, it will happen today. I will be in my class and the blood will start running down my legs and in the middle of it there will be a shapeless mass of tissue, the thing that isn't growing into a child.

My body didn't know how to get pregnant and it didn't know how to not be pregnant either.

I was for all practical purposes a pregnant woman. My breasts were tender. The mystery smells in my garbage disposal made me retch. I ate constantly to stave off nausea. I went to bed at 7:00 at night. And I waited for the blood that never came.

When we spoke, the doctor had told me it would probably happen within two weeks. When that first sonogram didn't show the embryo, she told me, it's not over until it's over, there's a chance it might be pressed up against the sac wall, we'll take another look in a week. She eased me into loss the way I imagined she would deliver a child into the world, her hands open and gloved.

I was pregnant but I wasn't carrying a child. What else is there to say?

~

The dark-haired boy followed me everywhere. He sat in the back seat of the car as I drove to work; he trailed behind me across campus, on the way to my office. I saw him out of the corner of my eye. He was maybe three or four, with beautiful mahogany curls. He wore shorts and fisherman sandals; sometimes he carried a satchel, like a boy going to school in another era. He was as real to me as the dead weight in my uterus. My phantom son.

He was a child who wanted a mother. He demanded French toast on Sunday mornings, so at 7:00 am I got into the car and drove to the supermarket. I bought white bread and half a dozen eggs, real maple syrup and a pint of milk. In the kitchen I assembled the ingredients on the counter while he sat beside me, dipping each piece of bread into the egg mixture. I fried them up and stacked them on a plate and we ate together in silence. When we were done we washed our hands, and I took a paper towel and wiped his sticky mouth.

On the couch I read to him a favorite childhood book, *Are You My Mother?*

"Who are you?" I asked.

~

There is a bottle of Naproxen on my bedside table for when the cramps come, whenever they finally do. I wait for them. I wait for the blood. My body is heavy with grief. Every night alone, I say the Mourner's Kaddish, this long year of loss.

My mother calls to tell me my grandfather has died on his way to a wedding. Someone uses the defibrillator in the airport while they wait for an ambulance where he is pronounced brain dead. After the funeral, we look at pictures of a cousin's new baby, and I cry.

I say the Mourner's Kaddish.

I take my little cat in for a dental cleaning, and she stops eating. For six days, I force her to drink with a medicine dropper. I warm her with a heating pad and sleep curled around her carrier. When her back leg stops working, I drive with her down the highway to the emergency vet, crying, *please don't die please don't die please don't die.* Her heart is too big, and she is drowning. When the vet tells me, over the phone, that she is gone, I hang up and scream.

Every night, *Yitgadal v'yitkadash sh'mei raba.*

Before we go home for Thanksgiving Dr. Boy fucks me for what I know will be the last time. Has he ever fucked a pregnant woman? My breasts swell in his hands. I hate him and I hate myself.

Even with his body slamming into mine I do not bleed.

Morning and night, I say Kaddish. I cry for everyone I have lost. I cry for my grandmother, I cry for my grandfather, I cry for my little cat. This long year, punctuated by loss.

My Ph.D. dissertation was on loss and melancholia in contemporary American fiction; even now, in the thick of sorrow, the irony is not lost on me. I wear black every day. Are you mourning, my students ask?

I will call you in a prescription, Dr. C says, you will need something for the pain. I take the pills and sleep the sleep of the depressed. She's been right about everything all along.

~

Home for the holiday weekend, I take the train into Chicago. For as long as I can remember—probably since high school graduation—I have seen my best friend Lynn the day after Thanksgiving. Today it is November 29, my thirtieth birthday. The West line chugs through the suburbs, from the small, quaint town where we grew up together over tea parties and basement sleepovers to the platform in Northwestern Station downtown. High school kids in baggy jeans and khaki-clad families crowd the cars. I think, how simple life was once, when the worst thing I could imagine was not getting the lead role in the winter musical.

I cry the whole way there, writing in my notebook. We pass Lombard, Maywood, Oak Park. I ignore the mother and toddler crammed in the seat across from me. It has been two weeks since the diagnosis, two weeks of carrying my not-quite child.

When the train arrives at the station, I find Lynn waiting for me at the bottom of the escalator; her red coat brightens the morning like a Christmas ornament. She hugs me tight, and we walk out into the city dusted with snow. I follow her down busy streets, on to the platform for the El where we wait for a train, and then back to her apartment. Once, years ago, she'd shown up on my mother's doorstep in the dark wearing only her nightgown and trench coat, her boyfriend hovering at her side. I'm moving out, she said, I just needed to tell you I'm moving out. She'd never gone back to the suburbs for more than a night. Now she is my lighthouse, my guide through the storm.

As we sip hot chocolate in the café across from her building, I tell her about the little boy. I can feel him now, pressed up against me. "He follows me around everywhere." I keep my hand on my belly as I talk, my gray wool sweater covering my unbuttoned jeans. The last time I'd been at the clinic Mary put her hand there gently and said, "You've gained weight. You are very pregnant." Didn't she understand there would be no child, that my abdomen swelled only with grief?

"You know me, Lynn. I'm not a person who believes in ghosts. I don't think I even believe in God. I guess this is just my way of making sense of what's happening to me."

She takes a bite of her muffin. Usually our conversations are colored with her anecdotes, glorious winding tales about characters she'd met at the bookstore or the people who worked in the cubicles next to hers at her day job or her brother's schemes to practice yoga on an organic farm in South America. Today it is my turn.

"I named him. I thought about it for a long time. You remember my cousin, the one who had cerebral palsy and died last spring? I gave him his name, Benjamin. Benjamin Matthew."

Matthew was our high school classmate and the man Lynn had almost married. They'd been together and apart and together and apart, sharing a studio apartment downtown, and then one day last spring she'd called me on the phone and said, "Well, he finally did it." He'd turned thirty and killed himself.

"I don't know if that's okay, naming a child who won't live after two people in their memory. But it's the only thing that makes sense to me now. I always thought I'd have a girl. Now I can't imagine any other child but this boy."

I give Lynn the last Kleenex from my backpack. We take a handful of paper napkins from the café and walk through the city. Benjamin trots by my side, reaching for my open hand. Lynn puts us both on the train.

~

I can't find Benjamin anywhere. I look in all the usual places, behind the chairs, under the bed, on the patio where he knows he isn't supposed to go.

The phone call from Dr. C must have scared him. When the phone rings around 5:00, I know who it is before I pick up. We've been talking on the phone a lot—I talk to her more frequently than I talk to friends—going back and forth about what to do about this baby who won't be born in July. Missed abortion, the diagnosis on the checkout form said, as if I had forgotten to show up to an appointment to terminate a pregnancy. I like to think I want him so much that my hormones are overcome with desire.

"Well," she says, clearing her throat. "I really don't want to do surgery unless I have to. It's a simple procedure but there are always risks, including scarring, and that would make it harder for you to conceive. But it's also not safe to let this go on so long."

"So what do we do?"

"In cases of ectopic pregnancy we often use methotrexate. It's a chemo drug." The long pause between sentences is filled only with the sound of our coupled breaths. "I don't know, honestly, if it would work. I'll have to read up on applications for using it for intrauterine pregnancies. Your beta HCG level is quite high. How about we do this. We try it and if it doesn't work then we talk about the D&C."

"Okay," I whisper. She says she will call me tomorrow to

confirm but to pencil in Friday for the shot. Pencil it in, just another appointment in my planner, like a conversation with a student or a date with a friend. It has been almost three weeks since the diagnosis. I don't want Benjamin to leave. I wonder how long my body will hold on to him without intervention. I am more than nine weeks pregnant with a child who will never be.

When Friday comes, I sit in the bathroom outside the clinic waiting room for a long time. Nurses and patients come and go. I rub my belly through my loose black dress.

I don't want the pregnancy to end.

Eventually, I check myself in for the appointment. I take out some poems from my backpack, but the words turn dark as storm clouds.

Helen calls me back, and we walk to the procedure room in silence. She draws my blood to check my liver function and hormone levels. She records my pulse and blood pressure on a chart. She draws up a syringe. And then she asks me to sign a consent form, stating that I understand the drug could cause birth defects and fetal death.

Goodbye, my darling boy, I whisper, goodbye my lovely one. I know I will never see him again.

~

There is a beginning and an end, Mary says. You were at A—
yes, I jumped up and down—and there is a Z. She puts her
hand on my belly, swollen and new, empty like the stomach
of a starving child filled with nothing but air. Maybe she
says, palpating, maybe you are at L. Maybe you are at W,
it's difficult to say. What you have to remember is that you
were at A.

~

I keep trying to write this story. To write it is to go back into it, and I can't. It's not that I don't want to. I can't. The loss of a child is a story that cannot be told. All I know is this:

My beautiful dark-haired boy was gone. I was thirty and more alone than I had ever been.

Here are the facts: The shot didn't work. By the time the doctor opened me on the table, I was in last week of my first trimester. The miscarriage had dragged on for more than a month.

~

What I remember most about the D&C was my feet, cold and wooly in the stirrups, and I couldn't tell where they ended and the cloth that held them began.

I remember the drive to the clinic that morning with my friend Cara, making small talk about school and her holiday plans; I remember her handing the car keys to the parking attendant, the long elevator ride upstairs, and the longer wait in the clinic; I remember the nurse weighing me and taking my blood pressure, before she escorted me to the room where I'd first met my doctor months before. Today she brought me back to the sonogram room, and took a final solemn look at the sac, just a large black hole in the middle of my uterus. No baby.

In my notebook: the codes on the paperwork from my doctor. She gives it to me in an envelope to bring to the hospital across the street. NPO 9:00 am; NKDA; IV: Plasmalyte; Labs: CBC, bHCG; Med: Cefotan. I write this jumble of syllables so someday I will understand. Her full name, Dr. Catherine Ellen Williams, sits below mine on the band on my wrist; we are married in this awful drama of loss. This is the one outcome I never let myself imagine.

During the long ride on the gurney, Dr. C stood by my head, wearing blue scrubs. In the open V of her shirt, her skin was freckled, gradually shedding her summer tan. When the procedure was over, she checked on me in the recovery room, putting her hand on my forehead the way a mother might touch another woman's child; she asked if I was stubborn, my body desperately clinging to pieces of tissue that would never become a baby. She held me in her gaze, a desperate embrace.

I remember the way blood drizzled out of me in the hospital bathroom afterward and how I laughed, almost maniacally, and Cara called in to ask if I was okay. The spinal hadn't quite worn off; my torso flopped onto my knees like Raggedy Ann as I sat on the toilet. I laughed because if I started crying I don't think I would ever stop.

I remember the night sky on the long drive home, punctuated by Christmas lights in the distance. When we'd left for my appointment, the sun was just coming up.

Back at my apartment, I had the presence of mind to put a towel down on the couch before I sat, and Cara made me some canned soup before she left me there to stew in my own blood. Nona was home with family for the winter break. Dr. Boy had left, too, for Indiana. I was more alone than I had ever been.

I woke in the middle of the night, my belly a tight fist. In the bathroom, I gave birth to one blood clot after another, an awful curdled jelly, like mashed blackberries, and crawled back into bed to call my doctor.

On the phone the next morning, her voice wrapped around me like a warm blanket. "I heard you had a bad night." I wanted her to come sit with me in the dark room, two women who had created and lost a child together. And I remembered that she had a husband and a child of her own, and it was Christmas Eve and they would probably be with relatives to celebrate. And I was touched, even in the midst of it, I was touched that she took the time to call me.

~

First I waited for the blood to come, and then I waited for the blood to stop. I was still bleeding when I went back to work the first week of January. And then it stopped for a few days, maybe a week, and started again just in time for my checkup with doctor. I wore a shirt the color of ripe pomegranates for our appointment and a new pair of black pants, since my body didn't seem to know what size it wanted to be. I changed my pad every half hour. Dr. C put a new diagnosis in my chart and put me on iron supplements. Then she sent me to the lab to have my blood drawn. The vials collected on the counter.

I felt better, as she had promised, now that the hormones were out of my system. But feeling better was a relative term. After the new year, after the bleeding stopped, I walked on the treadmill mile after mile, half listening to the lyrics of an Erasure song and the thud thud thud of my steps as I walked. "Oh that I should be ever so lonely," words whispered on the CD. Only later would I realize that the title was "Rescue Me."

Night after night I sat on the couch, numbing myself with television. The first time I saw the shot of a gurney on *ER* I went to the bathroom to vomit. I remembered being pulled down the hall, Dr. C somewhere at my head and a jar of god knows what at my feet to be sent to pathology. There was a lot in my uterus she'd said. It looked like tomato soup. I kept dreaming about it. I lost my first child again and again.

~

Afterward, she asked me what it felt like, when I was lying there numb from the waist down and colder, I think, than I'd ever been, shivering under a pile of white blankets. She put her index finger on my arm and pressed and asked "did it feel like that?" and I said something, maybe "sort of, it's hard to explain," because I knew she would be horrified if I told her the truth. It felt like having someone take a stick and force it up inside your uterus and twist it around. Which was, I guess, exactly what she had done. Oh, I'm sure I didn't feel every-thing. Or maybe I didn't feel much of anything but imagined that I did. It wasn't pain that I felt, I wouldn't call it that, but an unbearable pressure. And I remember the whole time I wanted to open my mouth, I wanted to cry, I wanted to tell her to stop, but I couldn't.

She hadn't ever done the procedure on anyone who was awake. You'll need something, she insisted, calling in the anesthesiol-ogist for a spinal block. I couldn't imagine sleeping through it.

The anesthesiologist stood at my head, I remember that, and he was the only one who seemed to be paying attention to me lying there, my head, my face, not just the space between my legs where the baby who wouldn't grow was being forced out. I remember him asking "is everything okay?" and I was grateful because the words were stuck in my mouth like I was wearing a muzzle. I wanted to crawl out of my skin. The wires from the heart monitor draped across my neck felt like they were strangling me, and I wanted to yank the IV out of my hand. I felt it scratching my vein. And Dr. C said yes, and soon it would be over. All of it would be over.

What I didn't tell her was I started lactating a few days later. I didn't tell her because I thought she would be embarrassed for not telling me that it could happen. I didn't tell her because it didn't seem particularly relevant to her job, which was getting me pregnant again. I didn't tell her because I didn't want to acknowledge my body's failing and its triumph, that it couldn't grow a baby but it certainly knew how to feed one once it got here. Small droplets of golden milk on my T-shirt after I showered. This child was so small he couldn't even be seen on a sonogram, but still he changed everything about me. My hormones. My temperature. My heart rate. The size and shape of my breasts. My body was unrecognizable.

What I didn't tell her was, as awful as it was, I would do it all over again exactly the same way if I had a choice. It was the only thing during all those long months that was tangible and real. It was the only decision I controlled.

What I didn't tell her, not with my voice anyway, was thank you for calling.

~

2.

IT WAS A HARD WINTER. Though it never snowed more than an inch, ice coated the streets and bridges from a series of storms, and I wondered if I'd ever go anywhere again. On TV, the local news showed one car sliding into another, mere blocks from the clinic. I was a passenger on a plane in a holding pattern, circling the Oklahoma Panhandle, desperately hoping to make my connecting flight.

Three months off, Dr. C had said, checking off more tests on a requisition form, thyroid function and natural killer cells, antinuclear antibodies, antiphospholipid antibodies, nine vials in all. My life stood still, like my car with its doors frozen shut in the campus parking lot.

Do you think, she'd asked me that day in the recovery room, her hand praying against my forehead, do you think it's been so hard because you're doing this alone? Her voice was soft, motherly. In a few minutes, she'd leave me and go home to her own family. Wrap Christmas presents, bake cookies with her daughter. Her question punched the tender spot in my abdomen. If I had a husband, he would have held my hand before the anesthesiologist inserted the IV; if I had a husband, he would have cried with me in the sonogram room, or written a poem about the child who wouldn't be born; if I had a husband, he would have taken me home after the procedure and tucked me into bed. If I had a husband, nothing about the experience would have been the same. I clung to her voice because she was the closest thing this baby had to a father. I wore grief like a winter coat I couldn't shrug off.

Was it harder because I was alone? Of course there was no way to know. I'd wanted this baby so I wouldn't be alone, so I would always have someone with me. A dance partner, a comrade in arms, so at night there was the sound of someone else breathing in the dark. I had tried to create a family for myself, and I had failed. I wasn't a person who accepted failure. I wanted to call up the Cryobank, order some more samples, and try again. It was fall when I'd gotten pregnant, the leaves just beginning to turn. By the time the doctor let me try again, the ice had thawed, and the crocuses had burst through the ground.

Valentine's Day. While my students picked up packages and flowers were delivered to campus offices, I drove down the highway in my black suit. It still didn't fit, but I sucked in my waist until the zipper mostly closed, added a safety pin to fasten it and a raspberry colored shirt to hide the pin, getting dressed for the closest thing I had to a date. An appointment for my annual exam with Dr. C.

I drove slowly, remembering the trip my senior English class had taken to see *The Importance of Being Ernest* in Chicago, the eight hours on the highway on the way home, being picked up at 10:00 at night by our parents who waited in their cars, squinting anxiously through frosted windshields until the bus pulled into the parking lot. That morning, on the forty-minute bus drive into the city, we'd said, wouldn't it be great if we missed last-period chemistry? Lynn and I read the twelve-page love letter a wannabe boyfriend had slid in the slats of my locker before school, the similes cloying as the candy hearts that accompanied them. That winter my biggest tragedy was not getting the lead in the high school musical, which wasn't really a surprise as I couldn't carry a tune.

I drove slowly to the clinic, my hands clenched on the wheel. Erasure played on repeat on the car stereo. Past the hospital, where I lay on the table numb from the chest down, past the hospital where the doctor scooped my insides like an avocado, overly ripe, and sent them for pathology to be tested. There were two small angry scars on my left hand, from the IV. I wondered if they would ever go away.

Normal, she said on the phone afterward. *The cells were normal, no signs of a molar pregnancy.* (A snowy pattern on the sonogram, she'd said earlier, perhaps indicative of a problem.)

V-Day. My students sold cookies shaped like vulvas in the union and brought the leftovers to class. Last night, Nona and I sat through their performance of *The Vagina Monologues*, the theater bright with paintings for sale. Our Texas girls dressed in pink and red. They wore feather boas and top hats. They took back the night, decorated cookies with pink frosting and paint. Driving down the highway, I thought, if my vagina had a monologue, this would be it.

In the lobby of the clinic, the woman who greeted patients was noticeably pregnant. If I hadn't had the miscarriage, I would have been twenty weeks along. She pushed the elevator button and rode with me up to the women's clinic. I dug my fingernails into my palms.

"Hey, Robin," said Dr. C, like we were old friends. Under her lab coat, she wore a gray pleated skirt that swished when she walked past. Her heels clacked against the floor. She didn't look like the person who had cut a child from my body, wearing blue scrubs and booties that covered her shoes, only her eyes visible over the surgical mask. Today she was Catherine, a woman who was once a girl like my students who had grown up in small town Texas, who had swapped Valentine hearts with friends. I wondered what she would have thought of those vagina cookies. I wondered if tonight, after she had seen all her patients and picked her kid up from school, her husband would take her to dinner and hold her hand.

"Hey," I said, from the scale. I turned my back so I couldn't see the number. Even if I never got pregnant again, my body was changed, irrevocably.

I joined my doctor in another one of those bland offices with a couple chairs and a small desk with a computer. The computer was new.

"So, how are you?" she said in a voice that was a bit too cheery. I liked her. I checked the sarcasm.

Her fingers danced on the keyboard. "Well, let's take stock." And she started, again, reviewing the narrative of the past year, a narrative as twisted and familiar as a fairy tale. "You did six cycles: three unmedicated, three monitored with Clomid, resulting in successful pregnancy in October, missed abortion leading to D&C in December, pathology normal, autoimmune testing in January positive for antiphospholipid antibodies." She did it without looking at my chart.

"So," she said, sitting back in the burgundy chair. "When do you want to start trying again?"

"As soon as I can. I mean, that's what I wanted to talk to you about."

"Well," she paused, toying with the gold charm at her throat. "You really need to take three whole cycles off, and that doesn't count the bleeding after the D&C. Other doctors will say you can try sooner, but there really is increased risk of miscarriage. And you've been, your body has been, through so much."

I clenched my fist until the nails dug dark crescent moons into my hand. It was the one thing that could keep me from crying. "So, the end of next month," I said.

"I think we should talk about injectables."

It was the logical next step in the staircase of fertility treatment. Unmedicated cycles, Clomid cycles, injectable cycles, then on to IVF. "But Clomid worked," I heard myself say. Some women I knew online spent thousands of dollars on injectable meds alone, swapping drugs with other fertility patients and even ordering them black market from Italy.

"Well, if you got pregnant and stayed pregnant we would say Clomid worked."

I swallowed hard.

She stared me down and cleared her throat. "Clomid is easy, I know. But it has risks, especially for a woman your size. If used repeatedly it thins the uterine lining too much. It's not really designed for small women. And I want to minimize the possibility of twins."

"But I thought injectables increased likelihood of multiples." Somewhere, in all my paperwork from the clinic, I still have the first chart she'd ever drawn me, showing odds of conception and multiple births on various protocols. Injectables were heavy hitting, big time drugs, the kind of drugs that, in the wrong hands, allowed for triplets and higher order multiples, like the septuplets that were always in the news.

"Yes, that's generally true. But what I want to do is a low-dose protocol starting later in your cycle. It's designed to improve the quality of ovulation, not the quantity of eggs. Should help boost your progesterone level, too." It sounded like she didn't trust my body. I didn't either.

"I don't know. I mean, a year ago I wasn't ready to consider Clomid."

"What are you afraid of?"

"I don't know. Twins, I guess."

"We just talked about that. The last thing I want is for you to conceive twins. There's already enough that puts you at increased risk for miscarriage." She tipped her head toward my file. "What else?" She looked at me skeptically. "You *can't* be afraid of the shots."

What I didn't want to tell her was fertility patients took injectables—real fertility patients, those who spent years trying to get pregnant before they found their way to her office, not me, not a thirty-year-old who never really tried to conceive in any systematic way but had the convenient diagnosis of "infertility" merely because of the lack of sperm and wickedly low progesterone. What she was telling me was she really thought I needed help getting pregnant and staying pregnant. It was a whole different game than eleven months ago when I sat in her office and she said, cheerily, "Who knows, you might be Fertile Myrtle."

"Robin," she took her glasses off. They dangled from a chain around her neck. "You made a decision at twenty-nine to get pregnant and raise a child on your own." She cleared her throat again, searching for words. "That's bold."

I nodded. It was the closest thing to a compliment she'd ever said to me.

"That's the hard part. Injectables?" She shrugged. "You can do this."

"Okay." The word caught in my throat.

She smiled and turned to the computer. I thought once she must have been a cheerleader, her long hair in ponytails, back in small town where she grew up. "What else? Helen left a note here to talk to you about the APA."

"Yeah. I sort of freaked out on her when she called to tell me. I mean, I know I asked to be tested for all that stuff, but I didn't really think that anything would be positive."

"Well, it's good that we tested you. Left untreated, research indicates up to 80% chance of miscarriage or fetal death." Her statistics were inline with what I'd read, scouring medical websites for information. "Now, there is a 5% false positive rate, but that's not a risk that I'm willing to take. We know about it, we treat it. Standard protocol is heparin and baby aspirin, starting after the IUI. It would be up to your OB how long to keep you on heparin; my recommendation would be the entire pregnancy. And you would probably be monitored closely to check fetal development."

I bit my lip. I thought, if I say anything I will cry. Not now, not now, not now.

In the exam room I put my feet in the stirrups. In the exam

room, she palpates my breasts, my abdomen, my uterus, with her gloved hands. She has touched me more times in the past year than my lover.

"You're from up North, aren't you? You must be used to weather like this."

I can't stop looking at her hands, the blue veins and freckled skin. Two months ago, the words stick in my throat, two months ago, in her blue scrubs. I am raw, exposed. I can't meet her gaze. "Yeah. The Chicago suburbs."

"How'd you end up in Texas?" She talks to me like we are new friends, getting to know each other over coffee at the bakery down the street.

"The job. I'm in a field you don't really turn down job offers. I like it. The job. My students are great. My colleagues. But I'd like to move home someday."

"Everything looks good," she says, peeling off her gloves and tossing them into the trash.

I sit up, holding the gown closed at my throat.

"So next month?" she says.

"Yeah. Next month."

"Okay." She smiles. Her teeth are small and white as a toothpaste commercial. "Talk to Helen about ordering the drugs. I'll give her a script for Repronex. And you should schedule a shot class. You'll be doing heparin subcutaneously, and the Repronex is intramuscular."

"Oh, the shots aren't a problem. Can't I just do it in my thigh? That's what I've been doing."

Her mouth opens in astonishment. "Doesn't that hurt?!"

I shrug. Don't shots always hurt?

"You really should do it in the glutes. Trust me."

"How?"

"You do yoga, don't you?" She turns, reaching across her torso, putting her left hand on her right hip. The world turns with her, twisting her head until she can see her right hand, holding an imaginary syringe and pushing the plunger in. The day turns from dismal to comic, and the formalities that separate us, doctor and patient, evaporate into Valentine's charm. "Oh, you can do this," she says, coaxing, the way a mother might talk to her obstinate child.

I think, in another time and place, under different circumstances, I could have loved her. Maybe I already do.

All I can do is smile. "I'll give it a shot." We laugh, co-conspirators, and she sends me out into Texas winter. My cheeks flush, pink with possibility.

If this were fiction, if I could write this story any way I want, I would leave out most of the winter. I would ignore the days I cried behind closed office doors, and the nights of self-pity, drinking colored drinks that gave me headaches and smashing glass on the porch. It was trite. All I needed was a freezer that gave out endless cartons of Ben and Jerry's ice cream and I'd be every depressed girl in every Hollywood film. Only those girls were usually depressed about men, not about having babies. I don't know any movies about women not having babies, not really, because not having babies is really boring, when the heroine isn't smashing glass on the porch. Other than that, it's a lot of time in doctor's offices and waiting rooms stacked with magazines about babies, and a lot of vials of blood stopped with rubber caps.

In my introductory literature classes I talk to my students about what makes a good story or, really, they talk to me about it. Plot, they shout. Car crashes and conflicts, chase scenes with cops. The girl wants the guy; the girl can't have the guy; of course in the end the girl ends up with the guy. It makes for lovely fiction.

But what happens when the story is true? What happens when the heroine decides at twenty-seven she wants to be a single mom and she finally gets pregnant and then she has a long drawn out miscarriage and spends a couple months being depressed? What kind of story is that?

I've always liked the bloopers and gag reels and outtakes from movies, seeing the behind-the-scenes banter of the actors getting ready to play their parts, where horror becomes slapstick comedy. It would be easy to sing this one note.

If this were a film, there would be a montage set to moody music, a series of melancholy shots. A woman dressed in black driving down the highway. A woman in black in her bathroom, filling a syringe. A woman in black standing in the lecture hall. A woman in black getting her blood drawn.

Still, there were moments that were wildly funny, like the time Dr. Pretty said Dr. C might want me to have sex after my HCG shot. I stared at him, dumb. What did sex have to do with me getting pregnant? "Oh," I finally said, "you know I'm using an anonymous donor, right?"

"Hey, Robin, I just talked to Dr. Williams about you. Here's the gab: ½ amp Repronex, starting day 6 of your cycle, bloodwork and sono on day 8 to see how things are going. Give us a call with any questions."

The new plan involved shots. Lots and lots of shots. I had enough needles, I thought, to supply the entire town. They came in a large box, individually wrapped in plastic, along with a small box filled with teeny tiny vials of injectable drugs. I kept them in the top drawer in my bathroom, with a bottle of prenatal vitamins, and my paperwork from the clinic.

Treatment for Patients with Antiphospholipid Syndrome (updated 2000). Dosage of heparin to be increased throughout pregnancy. Platelet count and calcium level monitored. Monthly sonograms to check fetal development. Increased risk of stillbirth. Increased risk of postpartum stroke. Heparin to be stopped prior to induction of labor and re-commenced twelve hours after birth.

Day 3: The first time back in the sonogram room, my chest

gallops with panic. My cheeks are cool; the coffee and breakfast bar I ate in the car turn over in my stomach. There is a new nurse, maybe Connie is her name, and she asks if I am sick.

Have you read my file? I want to say. Do you know what happened, the last time I was here?

On the way out, I see Dr. C, whom I have never seen at the clinic in the morning, doing some paperwork at a desk. She takes a sip of water, sees me pass her in the hall.

"It will be okay," she says. "Trust me."

Day 6: I go out for a margarita with Nona and Cara. We share a basket of chips and salsa, lick salt from the rim of the glass. In the morning, I wake up hung over, take my vitamins, and give myself a shot. I hit a capillary. Blood runs down my thigh.

Those long months of trying recorded in my journal. Notes about my symptoms, half-written poems scrawled in the waiting room of the clinic. Daily, I post messages to an on-line support group for women trying to become pregnant. We share our stories.

We talk about what we ate and what we drank and the timing of our IUIs and whether to take Clomid or injectables or move on to IVF. We talk about progesterone and spotting. We talk about what we do during those twenty minutes with our legs in the air, waiting for sperm to meet up with egg.

In the posts, I can shape my story how I want, turn tragedy into humor. It is a space where I can talk, any time day or night, a space where I don't need to hide my body beneath ill-fitting suits. In the posts, I sound stronger than I feel. Every time another woman sends a message about a new pregnancy, I think why not me? I hate myself for it.

"Are you okay?" Helen asks, her gloved hand fiddling with the speculum. "There's an awful lot of sighing going on up there."

To: Single Moms in the Making
From: RobinS@babynow.com
Subject: lots and lots of shots

One down and at least twenty-seven more to go. That would be
the number of pinpricks in the place I am hereafter referring to
as The Heparin Pouch. I think I'm starting to be glad for those
five pounds I never lost after the miscarriage. (And who said that
subcutaneous injections don't hurt?!)

And boy was my mother pleased when I told her that heparin
was made from pig intestines; my Kosher grandparents would
be so proud...

On the upside, I'm getting quite efficient at getting small quantities
of liquid out of miniscule vials.

Robin, 30, 1 m/c, APA+, 1dpo on 2ww #7

I didn't believe in fate. I didn't believe in "it will happen when
it is supposed to happen." I didn't believe I lost a child so I
could have the one I was meant to have. I didn't believe in
anything but the drive.

While driving I made lists of baby names, while driving I gave
imaginary lectures to my students, while driving I thought
about my father, while driving I thought about my mother,
while driving I wrote drafts of poems, while driving I wondered
how long I would keep driving.

"Oh my God," Nona said. "You look like a user." I was
covered in bruises. I'd given up on the shot in the butt after I
hurt myself so badly I could hardly walk. This time my thigh
had bruised blue purple, and the pooch of my lower abdomen
was a line of green blue and purple from the heparin. I looked

like I'd been beaten up in the playground after school.

I was in the bathroom with my shirt up and the needle cap in my mouth while my students got ready to do their poetry reading. I remembered my college roommate donning a similar pose, as she sat on the floor next to the mini fridge we had acquired after she learned she had diabetes and subsequently decorated our room with used syringes. Even the orange caps were the same. The 7:00 chimes rang out from the bell tower.

"How long do you have to keep doing this?" she asked.

"Every twelve hours for the next two weeks, or, if I get pregnant, until after delivery." My whole day revolved around these two injections. It's important, Dr. C had said, to keep your level consistent to avoid clotting.

It was April again, and I felt lighter than I had in a long time, my body humming with artificial hormones. I had a new donor again, one who shared my blood type. Bachelor #3 was also a science guy who worked on MS or something; I couldn't quite remember what he'd said on the CD. He was Irish, with green eyes, like a man I'd once loved, and that seemed to me just right. But, really, by now I didn't give choosing a donor that much thought; all that mattered was a clean medical history and whether or not he got me pregnant with a keeper.

The florescent lights buzzed overhead. In the mirror, my eyes were bright, my lips painted red, like a woman going on a date. I buttoned my skirt and we headed back to the auditorium, following the nervous chatter of my young poets. I couldn't wait to take a pregnancy test.

Lee would have liked the teeny tiny vials lined up in the drawer in my bathroom, the individually wrapped needles that reminded me of white plastic forks from take out Chinese. She would have liked the adventure, the covert ops, when I'd sneak out of campus events for a dose of injectable drugs. She would have laughed at Dr. Probe and asked Dr. Pretty out on a date, flinging her long ginger hair over her shoulder. She would have liked the row of bruises on my belly, the limp I had for a few days each month when my thigh muscles seized from the shots. But Lee was done with me.

I missed her wedding for a chance at happiness. I'd put everything else on hold for the baby, assuming it would all be there when I returned from the journey. I was wrong. She'd been there for me when the Baby Plan was just that, a hypothetical plan, something to whisper about over sickly sweet Thai iced tea. When it was real, when it was a big bloody mess, she was done. I didn't blame her. I thought about her every day, imagined where she was living and what she was doing, but I didn't blame her. I read her break up note and added it to the pile of evidence that said I was really, truly alone.

Even the nurses call me the human pincushion. Pinpricks in my belly, pinpricks in my thighs, pinpricks in the veins in my arms. They test my blood for estradiol, for progesterone, for human chorionic gonadotropin. They test my platelet count and clotting times.

Every month, a few days after the IUI, I start spotting. Dr. C cuts my dosage of heparin in half. Every month I run a low-grade fever, with no other symptoms of illness. She checks my white cell count; perhaps my body is under siege.

In April I make an appointment for June, to talk about moving on to IVF.

Joanna gave me a book about yoga and healing. On the massage table, she kneaded my hips and shoulders like dough. She released the pain.

To: Single Moms in the Making
From: RobinS@babynow.com
Subject: Clomid, my old friend

Well, in all the early-cycle excitement of picking out a new donor and agreeing on a protocol I like (yay! no more Repronex for me!), I'd forgotten about the <ahem> joys of Clomid. Like otherwise inexplicable moodiness. My poor students. No one should ever grade papers under the influence of fertility drugs. My ovaries are itchy, and I'm crying about what the light looks like on the apartment floor. I'm irrationally considering getting a kitten and calling it Mallomar. Oh boy.

All I can say is this: in 2.5 weeks I will be done teaching for the semester and I will know if I'm pregnant. Two more nights of Clomid to go...

Robin, 1 m/c, cycle #9 (4th on Clomid)

Every May, at every college I'd ever been to, campuses hummed with caffeine and end-of-the-semester projects. Here, students sprawled on beach towels on the quad, studying for their exams and working on their tans. Footballs and Frisbees arced over them. The sororities took out their cans of paint; their names colored the concrete on the path to the library. Faculty held classes under shady trees, drinking water from insulated mugs as they talked about Byron and Freud. Every seat at every computer lab was full of girls with their hair in makeshift buns, frantically typing papers due in the next half hour. Stress was thick as pollen in the air. I remembered my own student days fondly, staying up until two in the morning and then waking at five to finish papers, working them through sentence by sentence, going down to the cafeteria for cereal or a Pop Tart and then walking across campus, my sneakers damp. The library was open all night, students sipping Mountain Dew or black coffee to keep themselves awake.

In the evenings buildings sparkled with chandeliers lit for awards ceremonies; my colleagues and I donned our mortarboards and black gowns and the colored hoods that designated our discipline and alma mater and walked one after another in the order we were hired to take our seats in the chapel. The choir sang. Students in high heels accepted certificates for outstanding student in English, in History, in Mathematics. The president announced who was going to graduate school and who had accepted an internship and who had joined the Peace Corps. The faculty cheered.

Those last weeks of the term, we read honors theses and graded papers and wrote syllabi for the fall. We went out for lunch, five crammed in a car, swapping stories about our students over chicken salad sandwiches and black bean soup. My days were so full there was little time to think, let alone wallow in depression and self-pity; there were committee meetings and junior faculty meetings and department meetings about redesigning the curriculum. There were meetings of the whole faculty in the large lecture hall in the Administration building; Cara and I sat in the back and passed notes, our colleagues graded quizzes and did the crossword puzzle to pass the time. There were guest lecturers and seminars on sexual harassment. There were Saturday afternoons of shaking parents' hands and frantic emails from advisees who decided to drop out of school.

I'd come to Texas for a job. And now, with everything behind the scenes falling apart, the job was what I hung on to, a raft that kept me afloat. It was easy to get swallowed up in all that needed to be done. I recorded my blood tests on my calendar, alongside the letters of recommendation I needed to write. Those tulip-colored weeks, it was almost possible to imagine the job was enough.

In the conference room, Karen rolled her shirtsleeve and showed off the row of red marks from allergy shots. Grayson mumbled something about being on blood thinners. My left arm bore its signature gauze pad covered with tape; today it was progesterone testing. It was like we were sitting in the waiting room of a doctor's office or the common area of an old folks home. I looked at Nona and tried not to laugh. I wondered when I would run into one of my colleagues at the lab. I was always scheduling doctor's appointments around faculty meetings, worrying about last minute changes to the schedule. I felt like I was always in two places, on campus and at the clinic, my blood being drawn or having a procedure or talking to Dr. C. After next week, I thought, after we settled on curriculum changes and went our separate ways for the summer, maybe I wouldn't feel so divided and secretive.

It was strange, how much I wanted summer. I hadn't liked summer vacation until my senior year in college. As a kid, I'd been forced to play outside and go to various camps, doped up on antihistamines, where my arms still swelled with mosquito bites. I hated the popsicle stick crafts and the swimming, the chlorinated water stinging my eyes. Unscheduled days, I took my book with me to pick berries in the woods across from the elementary school; I dressed Barbies with neighbor friends sitting on the front stoop. Then, when I was older, there were the summers of vacuous jobs, serving French fries at McDonalds or making phone calls to sell newspaper subscriptions, because my parents wanted me to learn something about what they referred to as "the real world." In college one summer I worked on the first floor of the main branch of the library, shelving philosophy books, and, then, after my classes were done I'd head over to the children's department at the public library to staff their summer reading program. It wasn't until that summer, the summer before my senior year, the first summer I didn't go home for any length of time, that I learned how liberating long expanses of quiet time could be. Now, now I craved it.

My colleagues sat around the table in the conference room with their legal pads and their manila file folders, their black pens. It was good to have something to concentrate on. My latest chat with Dr. C had been less than encouraging. Repronex hadn't worked; it just made me ovulate early. The repeat stint at Clomid hadn't worked. We were running out of options.

"So," she said, folding her hands on top of my file, "are you ready to try in vitro? It's just taking you *so long* to conceive."

I watched her bat her eyelashes at the receptionist and get me an expedited appointment with the director of the IVF clinic. I was supposed to meet with him on Monday, so he could get me on the schedule for July. I tried to get my head around the fact that I wouldn't be her patient any more, that he'd be taking over my case. I would miss her.

I looked at the notes in my calendar, the circles representing my period and the squares for IUIs. I had Dr. C's business card paper-clipped to the day's date. On the back she'd scrawled *estradiol, PTT, PT, progesterone, platelets.* "Let's stop the baby aspirin and see if that makes a difference," she said when I told her I kept spotting. It was a throwaway cycle, anyway, just biding my time. I hadn't even used meds to stimulate follicle production; there was a large cyst on my ovary at my baseline sonogram—likely the residual effects of Clomid—and my blood estrogen level was too high. I was crushed, the same way I felt when I got a rejection from a literary magazine within days of submitting my poems.

"Sorry," Dr. C said on the phone, "I know it's hard to skip a cycle, especially when you've got the time off from work. But we really can't use drugs; it wouldn't work, and it could damage your ovary."

"How about an unmedicated cycle?" I asked. I couldn't take a month off, not this month, not when I'd given up another friend's wedding.

"Sure," she said. "That could work."

I might as well have thrown a thousand dollars in the trash, I thought. The timing was awful. I'd gotten a natural LH surge on the ovulation test kit before I had time to do a trigger shot, the sole purpose of which was to insure that the sperm showed up just before the egg.

I closed my planner, took out my notes from the last department meeting. The words were fuzzy. My head hurt. I rubbed my temples. All I wanted to do was go back to my air-conditioned apartment and sleep until next week.

A bee worried its way through the hole in the screen and walked around the seminar table. It happened every spring.

"So," Ron said, setting his books down on the table. "Why don't we get started."

After a week trapped in the conference room hammering out a new curriculum for our undergraduate major, Nona and I drove into the city, this time in her little silver car, Madonna on the stereo. We were released into the summer—to do our work, to see our friends, to gear up for a new year. Today we could have been any tourists new to the city, headed to the big farmer's market, to see the sights. Nona parked next to a line of Ford trucks with American flags waving from the antennae. I put on my floppy summer hat; it was already over ninety degrees, only 10:00 in the morning.

We wandered through the covered market, bell peppers and sweet vidalia onions in baskets, chili ristras and braided garlic bulbs hung from the ceiling. We sniffed bouquets of cilantro and basil. She bought a painted ceramic lizard to add to her collection on her bathroom wall. Little boys speaking Spanish raced through the aisles. We had lunch at a neighborhood restaurant outside, big burritos and iced teas, sharing chips and guacamole and conversation. We were blocks away from the clinic, but I wasn't a patient today. I couldn't remember the last time I'd been to the city and not having a medical procedure or my blood drawn.

"Talked to Dr. Boy lately?"

We didn't talk about Dr. Boy much. Whatever it was that defined the ins and outs of our relationship was too difficult to explain to others, without me sounding like an idiot. What I would have told any friend of mine who described the situation was *run away now.* Why I couldn't give myself that advice I hadn't quite figured out. Maybe it was as simple as I loved him.

"No. Actually I can't remember the last time he called, it's been so long." The last time I saw him I remembered all too well; it was the day before the D&C when, stupidly, I drove to see him and watched him pack his things for his trip home for Christmas. I put that on my mental list of things I'd never do again. "He just...well, he just hasn't been there for me, you know?"

She smiled a wistful smile and tightened the elastic band that held her hair. She and Sawyer were finally, officially, engaged. During the school year they saw each other twice a month, taking turns driving six hours to visit. Summer, he pretty much moved in with her, which meant I saw her about half as much. One thing Dr. Boy was right about was married folks and couples preferring to spend time alone. And Small Town Texas was no place for a single girl. Sometimes I wondered if the reason I wanted to have a baby was just so I wasn't alone in my apartment at night.

"Well," Nona said, pulling a credit card out of her wallet, "we've got all afternoon. What do you want to do?"

The official purpose for our outing was that we were picking up Sawyer from the airport. Well, she was picking him up and I was keeping her company. I had that old squinch owl feeling over my right eye. I'd had it a lot lately. The truth was, I didn't feel like doing much of anything.

When we left that morning, I thought that I spent all this time driving back and forth to the city, and I hadn't done much of anything fun. I hadn't been to the jazz clubs Dr. Boy talked about. I hadn't tried restaurants Cara and Alejandro talked about. There were things I wanted to do, check out the big art museum, see some historic sights. Nona had been in Texas half the time I had, and she'd seen about three times as much.

It was only lunchtime. I was enjoying her company. But all I wanted was to go home and sleep.

By the time we left the modern art museum and headed in the general direction of the airport, I had a raging headache. I bought a travel-sized package of Tylenol at a gas station and popped two in my mouth. "Is there enough for me?" Nona asked. It was sweltering, and neither of us had had much to drink all day.

We sat in her air-conditioned car in silence. I was out of words. I wanted to go home and take a long bath and climb into a bed with crisp laundered sheets. That morning I'd tossed another negative pregnancy test into the trash. The year could be summed up with that single image: a woman holding a plastic test strip in her hand, holding it up to the light, and then letting it fall into the trash. Sometimes, minutes later, she comes back and takes it out, willing the second line to appear. It does, the gray shadow of liquid evaporating on the test strip, not the pretty pink of a positive result.

We drove to the airport, past the off ramp I usually took to get to the clinic. It had been a whole year since my first IUI, when I went into the Baby Gap and declared that I was buying a purple outfit for my daughter. I had hardened since then. I'd lost too much in Texas.

I sat at my desk and looked at my notes. I got up and went to the kitchen and poured myself a glass of water. I went back to my desk and checked my email. I flipped through the table of contents for a book I was thinking of teaching in my gender studies class in the fall. I went into the bathroom and pulled a home pregnancy test from the box I kept under my sink. I bought them in bulk online; they were just the test paper without the fancy plastic wand, for less than a dollar apiece.

I peed in a cup and dipped the test strip and set it on the counter. I went back to my desk. I scanned the list of new posts on the single moms' board. I checked the clock. Five minutes had passed.

I peered at the test strip in the bathroom. Negative. Again.

I put on my sneakers and grabbed my keys and a water bottle. I drove down the farm road and past the line of churches and parked in the lot next to the outdoor track. Kids kicked soccer balls and turned cartwheels. Moms pushed babies in jogging strollers.

I walked fast, switching the water bottle from hand to hand. "I give it 80% chance it will work," Dr. IVF had said yesterday. "You are young, healthy. When your next cycle starts, give me a call and we can figure out when to put you on the schedule."

I was petrified. I emailed Dr. C when I got home from the appointment, asking for moral support. *Go for it!* she wrote back.

80percent80percent80percent. I chanted the statistic as my foot hit the gravel. This will work, this will work, this will work.

After I'd done two miles and ran out of water, I sat down on a metal bench and rested my jelly legs. I walked back to the car. A grasshopper stuck to the windshield. I carried it all the way home.

It would work. It had to.

If I hadn't lost the baby, my due date would have been less than a month away.

I tossed my keys on the kitchen counter and walked into the bathroom. Staring up at me from the counter was a test stick with two blurry pink lines.

To: Single Moms in the Making
From: robins@babynow.com
Re: A little luck from Ned the Gnome

Long story somewhat shorter: I just couldn't take it anymore. Yes, I broke down and peed on a stupid stick. One of those online cheapos. Minutes pass. Nothing. I left it on the counter and went for a walk around the park because this whole IVF thing has me too anxious to sit still. Well, half an hour or so later I got home and found a positive pregnancy test. Evaporation line, I thought. But I can't just leave it at that, I'm way too anxious and just want my period to start so I can get on with IVF. Pickup another test from

Wal-Mart. Yup, it's positive. So I guess I don't need to worry about IVF after all. It seems I am pregnant on the cycle that shouldn't have been. Hooray for playing my own doctor!

Robin, 30, 1 m/c, 3w6d pregnant!

P.S. Ned is a garden gnome I gave to the nurse the day of my IUI. See, giving nurses gifts really does work.

3.

A PERSON, IT SEEMED, had set up shop in my uterus. As soon as that second line appeared on the test strip, it all fell into place. The headaches, the funny taste in my mouth, the insomnia, the vegetable soup that tasted off at the restaurant. When I saw the two lines on the stick, all I could do was laugh. It wasn't real yet; I hadn't even taken a blood test. I got up and walked around the apartment, not sure what to do with myself. "Helen," I said when her voicemail picked up. "Put me on the schedule for a beta tomorrow? I got a positive HPT."

The highway, basking in early June sunlight, was sharp and clear when I drove to the clinic in the morning. My memories are fleeting and distinct as a slideshow of a beloved family vacation: the huge concrete supports for the new highway boasting the lone star of Texas, the elephant fountain dribbling water onto the grass, the tourniquet on my left arm. I went home to wait. The world seemed off balance and carnival bright. I went to the only place I really felt safe, a deep pocket of my mind where I was surrounded by those who knew me best.

I imagined Dr. C sitting wherever she sat when she talked to the nurses on the phone, sipping water from a plastic cup, when they told her, whichever one of them told her, that one of her patients was pregnant.

"Wonderful! Which one?"

"Robin Silbergleid."

"Robin? I thought we cancelled her cycle."

"No, just went unmedicated this time around."

151

"That's right, I forgot. I told her it could work! What's her beta?"

"188."

"Day 14?"

"13 or 14. She did two IUIs."

"Well, I'll be. This one's a keeper."

"Yeah, I thought you'd be happy to know." In my mind, she hangs up the phone and slips it back into her tote bag. She takes another sip of water from her cup, leaving a pink lipstick smile on the rim. In my mind, I am not just any other patient. I am someone she has taken an interest in, someone who fascinates her as much as her unknown life fascinates me.

I wanted to tell her myself. I wanted to tell her that it wasn't Clomid or Repronex or IVF. It was all me, my body, with a little help from a nurse who, it seemed, had just become a dad. It was all so new I couldn't do anything but put my hand against my belly like a toothy grin. I walked around the apartment and pet Pistachio and cried. I was going to be a mother. And this time it would work. It had to.

I went to yoga. I lay in savasana, corpse pose, my body surrounded by light. Joanna was talking us through deep relaxation, and the light touched me until everything melted with its warmth, my skin and bones and muscles, my ligaments and joints. I floated on the raft of her voice, energy radiating out from my uterus, still small as a piece of fruit and tucked well beneath my pubis bone. I melted into the floor. My whole body smiled.

When the chimes called us back to the waking moment, I helped fold up the mats and stack them against the wall. The other women chatted, gathering up purses and putting on shoes, and I felt very far away, in a world big enough to contain only me and this small child. I was happy. I was happy to be having a child and happy not to have to do IVF and they were separate but related happinesses.

I waited in the outer office for Joanna to finish talking to one of the other women about the class schedule, her plans to move the studio, the artwork she was doing on the side.

"You're pregnant," she said bluntly when everyone else had left. "When we were lying there in savasana, I thought, Robin is pregnant."

"You're amazing," I think I said, but I could feel it too, the energy coming off me in waves, and it was so different than last fall, when there was the heaviness and the blood, and I didn't want to think about the possibility that nine months from now I wouldn't have a child. The worst thing I could imagine was going through it all again, the miscarriage and the dark months off, and then trying again.

I thought of Joanna, who had told me she had lost children of her own. I had lost track of how many, three or four, with her different husbands. And how she had finally settled into step-motherhood gracefully, as she did everything, it seemed. She had grown into her life, into the yoga studio and her cabin in the woods, and I hoped that I could fill my own life as gracefully, as graciously. I want to tell her, now, what I don't think I ever managed to say. I think of you, and am astonished.

At home I sat on the couch and rested, and the light turned to darkness, in the windows outside the porch and in the unlit room around me. There was a dull ache in my pelvis that I didn't trust. At 8:00, I took my heparin shot and tossed the used syringe in a plastic salad container in the cabinet under my sink. I took my progesterone and calcium supplements with a glass of orange juice, and I fell asleep there, in my quiet home, my home that was starting to feel full again.

I loved Nona's pad thai more than just about anything in the world, but if I put another bite of those noodles in my mouth I was going to hurl. I shoved them around my plate and smiled and tried really hard not to smell them, just like in high school when I'd close my nostrils and breathe through my mouth in biology class.

"Want some more?" Sawyer said.

"No thanks. I'm good." I took slow sips of water. I was hard to do with my nose plugged up. I remembered swimming lessons when I was a child, the way the chlorine worked its way into my nasal passages. I felt sick.

I sat across from Frank, the college's lone music historian and the guy I had vaguely thought about asking out on a date when I was hopped up on hormone supplements. He was tall and wore wire-rimmed glasses and didn't look anything like the men I usually fell for. He was balding. He seemed a bit obsessive-compulsive, or at least Nona worried about cleaning her house before he came over because he had a tendency to point things out. As we sat there, I felt heat rise in me, my cheeks flushed with self-consciousness. I told myself it was probably just the extra estrogen pulsing my body. I was sure everyone could see it in my swelling breasts, the small rise of my abdomen. In a few months I would be a mother, and I didn't really need to worry about dating men anymore.

I'd realized sometime in those long months of thinking about getting pregnant and trying to get pregnant that the whole reason I'd dated men was because everyone knew that dating was the first step toward having a baby, which was the only thing I really ever wanted. Now I could be done with all that. Thank goodness.

A fresh wave of nausea crested in my throat, and I excused myself to the bathroom. I turned on the water and vomited into the toilet. When I was done retching, I washed my hands and rubbed cool water over the back of my neck and forehead. Then I returned to the table, where Frank and I exchanged small, toothless smiles. I took another sip of water, savoring the moment. I couldn't imagine feeling lighter.

"I know it's hard. But you've already had a miscarriage and

you're on heparin. Take it easy. Get your mind off it. Sit on the couch and watch some funny movies."

Dr. C and I were discussing the latest round of bleeding over the phone. It started the way it did the first time, just a few drops of red blood and then something heavier and foreboding. Again, I went to the clinic for a blood test, an early sonogram. Now all I could do was wait it out. Wait to see the embryo, wait to see the heartbeat, wait to make it through the first trimester. I circled dates on my calendar. I kept it taped to bathroom wall, along with my New Year's goals. Get pregnant. Stay pregnant. Write.

I sat in the old armchair next to the TV, where I'd once sat on Dr. Boy's lap, keeping an eye on Nick the Garden Gnome, who had finally made his way across the country to Texas. I was holding on to him until my sonogram, and then I'd send him to someone else in need of good fertility vibes. Baby dust, we called it. Apparently, my success had inspired a trend among my online friends trying to conceive. He watched over a pile of baby clothes on the floor. It was part of a still life I'd photographed, Nick with baby supplies, Nick with spent syringes. Pistachio glared at him, puffing up her tail.

"I'm supposed to go on a trip in a couple weeks. Is that going to be a problem?" While I talked, holding the cordless phone up to my ear, the cat batted at the gnome's head until he tipped over. I contemplated the energy it would take to get off the chair and move him to the counter by the cd player and decided against it. The progesterone, natural and synthetic, kept me woozy and doped up as if I'd overdosed on Benadryl.

"Really, I wouldn't suggest it for the first trimester. I mean, if it were your best friend's wedding or something, then maybe..."

I laughed. "Yeah, it's a wedding reception for my college roommate." I'd made the decision not to go to the wedding back when I was pregnant the first time, and due right around her the date of the wedding. Then I wasn't pregnant and decided not to go because I didn't want to miss a cycle. As it turned out, she got married and I got knocked up in the same weekend, which seemed fitting. But I didn't want to give up the chance to celebrate one of my dearest friends so I could sit on my couch in Texas and fret. I was scared, but I had enough sense to know that if I was going to miscarry, getting on a plane really wouldn't make any difference. Dr. C was taking every precaution.

"How's this? No spotting for two weeks. None. Then I'd feel a little more comfortable." I could hear a child's voice in the background as we talked, asking if she could watch TV. It hadn't occurred to me that she would call from home. "Jenny," she called, "I'm on the phone."

"Okay." I sighed heavily.

"There are no guarantees, you know that. But the odds really are in your favor."

"Thanks," I said.

"You can always call me at the office if you need to talk."

"Thank you. I appreciate that."

"It's going to be okay. Trust me." It occurred to me not for the first time that there wasn't a whole lot of difference between a psychotherapist and a reproductive endocrinologist when it came to the emotional drama of fertility treatment.

"Thanks. Have a good night."

"You too, Robin. You too."

My heart started racing during that last stretch on Sparrow, next to the house with the elephant fountain spraying water on the front lawn. I thought about everything I had learned about fertility treatment and human reproduction, I thought about the numbers, beta HCG and progesterone and estradiol. I thought about charts I'd seen on the internet, charts that gave a pregnancy with my beta levels—higher, it seemed, than many women having twins—95% chance of going full term. And then I thought about that Valentine's Day in Dr. C's office, talking about the antiphospholipid antibodies and—what had she said?—60 to 80% chance of miscarriage. I thought about that beautiful sac we'd seen just a week ago— exactly the size it should have been—the day I saw red blood and panicked. And I thought about that empty sac we'd seen months ago, when I learned my first pregnancy wasn't viable. Right now, the two experiences didn't feel much different.

The last mile seemed impossibly long. Finally, I reached the circle drive outside the clinic and left my car to be parked. I stood outside for a long minute, watching patients climb out of cars and settle into wheelchairs for the journey on the elevator and down the narrow hallways of the medical center. They were sick. They had cancer and rheumatoid arthritis and fibromyalgia. I was sick only with need.

I toyed with the straps of the summer bag I was using instead of my backpack and took a deep breath. I walked through the revolving door and across the gleaming tile floors of the lobby. The woman whose only job was, it seemed, to greet patients and push the elevator button was hugely pregnant, in a black knit dress stretched taught over her belly, a little white bow tucked under her breasts. For months, I'd watched her grow, her abdomen mocking me, escorting me up to the fifth floor where I sat, having my blood drawn and my ovaries examined. She always smiled, a big toothpaste ad smile.

When the elevator opened outside the fertility clinic, I checked myself in at the front desk and went back to sit with the other women waiting for sonograms in the row of chairs outside the nurse's station. We never talked to each other. Our faces all held the same uncertain look, hopeful and lost, not unlike puppies in their cages at the pound. Sometimes I read a literary magazine or graded blue book exams while I waited to be taken into the sonogram room. I liked the bustle of nurses going in and out, hushed laughter and conversation that reminded me of a coffee shop. I belonged here. I wasn't ready to be sent away. Months before, a woman had brought one of those giant cookies the size of a plate to give to the doctor who had impregnated her and then sent her happily on the way to an obstetrician across town. Only an optimist would have brought the cookie with her to her appointment; I supposed a pessimist would have brought a box of Kleenex. I brought the notebook I'd been keeping all year, compiling drafts of poems and lists of medical terms and baby names. When the woman seated next to me stood to ready herself for the march down to the sonogram room—I could see her bracing herself against disappointment—I took it out and worked on a draft of a pantoum. Blood was one of the repeating end words. I held it close as a touch stone.

The new nurse called me back. In the small bathroom, I took off my linen pants and folded them neatly on the chair. I wrapped myself in the paper gown and held it closed with my left hand while I opened the door with my right. Then I hopped onto the examining table, smoothed the sheet, and lay back. I rested my hands gently on the soft swell of my lower abdomen and closed my eyes. I listened to Joanna's voice in my head and tried to slow my heart rate.

There was a quick knock at the door, and Dr. Probe walked in followed by the nurse. The nurse sat down at the counter and made a few notes in my chart, while the doctor fiddled with the condom on the transducer. That part never ceased to amuse me, like the cartoon of an erect penis I'd seen at a science center during junior high.

He rooted around for a moment, an act that always reminded me of the worst parts of sex, but as soon as he stuck that wand inside me, I gasped.

There is no other way to say this. It was beautiful. A dark balloon smaller than a newborn's palm, with a pea-shaped white blur inside it. It looked like a flickering grain of barley, gritty and unclear. Heartbeat. Dr. Probe pushed some buttons on the computer and it started tracking the rhythm.

"That's perfect," Dr. Probe said, "everything looks perfect. The heart rate is exactly what we'd want at this stage."

I asked for a picture. When I miscarried, when I lost Benjamin, I'd thrown out the positive home test in a fit of rage. Sometimes I wondered if I'd ever been pregnant at all, and then I got bill for my D&C, coded as obstetrical care. I could see this baby, its heart beating beneath my own. Whatever happened, right now I was a mother to a thriving embryo.

He printed off two copies on slick paper, stuck one in my file for Dr. C, and gave the other to me. They left me alone in the sonogram room, my checkout papers on the counter. I hung on the insurance code like a lifeline. V23.9, Supervision of pregnancy, high risk.

Later, before I began the drive home, I sat at a nearby café eating rosemary potatoes, taking the sonogram picture in and out of the book I had tucked it in. Embryo with heartbeat, 6w2d.

The waiting room at the obstetrician's office looked like a stock scene from a movie, where the teenage heroine goes to get birth control and sits sandwiched between two hugely pregnant women. I'd never seen bellies swollen to such intimidating proportions. Some of the women had toddlers sitting at their feet, playing with dolls. The only one who wasn't visibly pregnant had a newborn in a stroller. I pulled my black tank top down over the elastic waist of my skirt and tried not to look at the other patients. On the side table there was a book labeled "Dr. Black's Babies," which, when I opened it, was full of pictures of a blue-gowned doctor standing next to proud fathers holding their swaddled newborns. There were a few of her balancing a baby on the palm of her hand in the operating room. And the obligatory Christmas photos, pony-tailed girls wearing red and green plaid dresses and boys in green sweaters and black pants. Something about it struck me as presumptuous. I still didn't quite believe I'd end up with a baby living in my house in about seven months. I put the photo album down and flipped through one of those parenting magazines with the celebrity mom gleaming on the cover, touting prenatal yoga or water birth. I stifled the impulse to mock it.

Before I had a chance to flip through the table of contents, a black-haired nurse opened the door and looked down at a clipboard. "Robin?"

I stood up and pulled my top down again. I really needed to get some new clothes.

"Follow me," she said, ushering me down the hall. The walls were painted a pale pink, and it reminded me of Victoria's Secret. One of my friends had told me that the pattern in the carpet was a bunch of vaginas. Subtle. "First, we need a sample and your weight. Then meet me back here."

On a small table in the bathroom, there was a stack of specimen cups for urine samples and a black permanent marker. There was also basket full of pantiliners and tampons. I supposed most of the women who were here needed either the cup or the tampon, or maybe both. On the back of the door hung a poster about prenatal nutrition. I realized, with a tinge of something that could only be described as homesickness, that the Anne Geddes' calendar from the sonogram room at Dr. C's would have fit right in.

When I was finished, the nurse was waiting for me right outside the door. "Weight?" she asked.

I'd already gained four pounds. A few more and I'd weigh more than I ever had in my life. I felt solid.

She recorded the number in my file and led me to the doctor's office, with a huge mahogany desk and a row of bookcases filled with medical texts and back issues of obstetrics journals. "The doctor will be right in."

I sat heavily into the oversized chair, already tired from drive and the waiting, since I'd arrived at my appointment half an hour early, when the whole office was closed for lunch. It was the student chair. I was usually the person on the other side of the desk. Award certificates and diplomas framed the desk, designed to reassure patients like me that I'd made the right choice coming here, almost an hour from home, instead of the local hospital where even a blood test seemed like a life-threatening procedure.

The door opened, and a woman with long frizzy hair came into the room. She wore pink scrubs, bright against the dimly lit room. "Hello," she said, "I'm Dr. Black." Her accent was saccharine as Texas tea.

She sat down and opened my file in what seemed like a single, well-choreographed movement. "I see," she said, her eyes scanning sheets of white paper with my name in bold letters at the top. "You've been down to the med school."

I nodded. That was a way of putting it.

"And you worked with Dr. Williams. Dr. Catherine Williams?"

"Yes," I said, "that's why I'm here."

"I know her."

"Yes," I repeated, imagining scenes where they got together for coffee at medical conferences, these two Southern blonde doctors who seemed to hold the key to my happiness.

"Here's a report from a sonogram, two days ago? Growth and heart rate both normal. And she has you on progesterone and heparin?" she asked, flipping through the faxed pages of my chart.

"Yes."

"And that's because of..." She paused, briefly, and I wondered if I was supposed to finish her sentence. "Antiphospholipid Syndrome," she said it without affect, like it was something she encountered every day. At least she'd heard of it before.

"Yes." I looked out the window at the green arch of the hospital across the street.

"I suppose that's the major thing we need to talk about. This is what we consider to be a high-risk pregnancy. Now, I have had patients with APA who've had no problem at all, but you need to be prepared for the possibility of long term bed rest, if the baby isn't growing well, and I definitely won't let you go past your due date." She rattled off a quick list of everything that could go wrong, saving maternal stroke and fetal death for last.

I covered my mouth and willed myself not to vomit on her desk.

Her speech sounded like she'd lifted it from the patient brochure I'd been given at the fertility clinic. How they'd increase my dose of heparin as the baby grew, monitor me with monthly sonograms and non-stress tests, and eventually induce labor, as early as thirty-seven weeks.

"In cases like these," she finished, "it's best to get the baby out of a hostile environment." The word swelled along with me. "You look a little queasy. Has nausea been a problem?"

I shrugged my shoulders. "A little." The nausea I could deal with; it was the instant and unpredictable need to vomit that I could have done without. That morning I'd thrown up just from brushing my teeth.

"I'll give you a list of things you can do to alleviate nausea. Ginger, peppermints, things like that. Now," she said, "let's go check you out," her voice a little too chipper at the prospect of getting me into stirrups and rooting around my cervix.

Between the consult and the physical exam and the insurance paperwork, the appointment took most of the afternoon. Then, she sent me with a test requisition to wait in the lab upstairs. In addition to everything else I was routinely tested for, Dr. Black wanted to make sure my calcium level wasn't too low, a common side effect of long term heparin use. In the lab, I gave the phlebotomist my right arm and looked away nonplussed. I'd used my left two days before.

"You have great veins," he said, snapping on a tourniquet and surveying the web of blue-green blood vessels readily apparent on the surface of my skin.

"Thanks," I joked. "That's about the only thing I've got going for me."

When I was all checked out, I took my bandaid arm and my plastic bag full of samples of prenatal vitamins and brochures for parenting magazines across town to the Whole Foods to stock up on ginger snaps. I ate them all day long; I even slept with the box on the extra pillow in my bed.

I was exhausted. I sat in the café sipping water and eating a fresh fruit tart from the bakery. I smiled at the students reading fat nursing textbooks and moms with toddlers and sippy cups. I took the latest sonogram picture out of my notebook and stared at it. At eight weeks, the baby was the size and shape of a kidney bean, growing a millimeter at a time. Another milestone to check off on my calendar. I took another bite of the tart, savoring each blueberry and bit of kiwi. It had been a good day. *Grow,* I whispered, *grow; I want to know you.*

4.

I WORE AN ELASTIC WAIST black skirt and a form-fitting camisole to see Dr. Boy. He was somewhere that summer, Paris, I think, and he'd just gotten home. For a reason I couldn't articulate, I really wanted him to see me pregnant, not so heavily pregnant that I was uncomfortable but the way I was now, early in the second trimester, my belly noticeably beginning to swell. I always ended up in his bed in August, and I remembered what someone had once told me, how close the word *sundress* is to *undress*.

"Wow," he said, putting his hand on the bump, "you're really pregnant."

"Yup," I said.

"Wow."

We sat together on his couch in the afternoon sun, copies of *Harper's* and *The New York Times Book Review* open on the coffee table, a stack of library books next to the TV. There were familiar framed prints on the walls of the living room, Modigliani and Romare Bearden, and I thought about my own bare walls, my old Georgia O'Keeffe "Light Iris" coiled around itself in a closet somewhere. Hanging pictures on the wall struck me as a symbol of permanence that I wasn't yet ready to accept.

He poured orange juice into plastic cups and we sat together, just two old friends, with a ball game as background on the TV. I hadn't seen him in months; now, pregnant with another man's child, being with him seemed safe again. The last time we'd had sex was a thirtieth birthday present of sorts, and it was full of tears and masochism, my body overcome with desire and loss. It was a couple weeks before the D&C, and I'd hoped vaguely I'd start bleeding in the same way that heavily pregnant women sometimes have sex to bring on labor. Now, sitting next to each other, his hand stroking my shoulders into submission, I thought about my old fantasy, the two of us living in a duplex and raising a child together, and I realized how happy I was, how perfectly content to have this baby, my own child, my immaculate conception, wiggling around in my uterus. I was happy to go home to my quiet apartment and my old cat, to lie down on my bed and listen to my child's heartbeat, my hand on my belly, waiting to feel the first movements from the outside.

But there was something in his eyes—something in the way that his long fingers felt wrapped around my growing abdomen—that felt possessive. In a way, he'd fathered this child, like a seed he'd planted but forgot to water. It sprouted inside me anyway. I wondered what he really thought about all this. Every time I found myself thinking of him, as I lay in a queen sized bed too big for just me, I told myself I wasn't going to sleep with him again unless we had a real conversation about having a committed, adult relationship, and, even then, I wasn't sure I would say yes. That vision of the two of us seemed as far away as a trip to France.

At dinnertime, I didn't wait for him to invite me to stay. I kissed his cheek and drove home to feed the cat and myself. I stopped at the Starbucks halfway between his place and mine, got a cup of decaffeinated iced tea and continued on the highway. Cher was singing on the radio, "A Different Kind of Love Song." And the baby thumped her foot against the wall of my uterus, keeping the beat.

I kept running into doors. I'd gotten huge, it seemed, just as we returned to school in the fall. I ran out of breath just walking across campus and trying to open the large door to the Humanities building. It was enough just to eat and grow this little person. I'd told all my colleagues over the course of the past couple weeks, after the first trimester was over and I'd had another sonogram, featuring a creature that looked more like a baby and less like an alien with a huge head and impossibly tiny limbs, its body grainy white against the black circle of amniotic fluid on the monitor.

I wondered how fast the gossip would spread. I felt like I was wearing one of those shirts that said "Baby," with an arrow pointing down, like Hester Prynne's scarlet letter. My cheeks were flushed, my belly round.

It was a small college in a small Texas town, where cheerleaders married their football star boyfriends right after high school graduation and gave birth to their first child just before their first anniversaries. The other women I knew in town were silver-haired beauty queens who wore pink lipstick to yoga class and picked up homemade lasagna from the gourmet shop in town if they weren't home on time to make dinner for their husbands. Or my female colleagues, like Karen, who were married to their jobs and went home at night to feed their animals and grade papers, a generation of women for whom professional success usually meant personal disappointment. Even for my students, bright young women who insisted they could be anything they wanted to be, reproductive choice largely meant access to birth control and putting unwanted children up for adoption. Picketers lined up in the strip mall outside the Planned Parenthood. What choice really meant, I wanted to tell them, was choosing if and when and how to have a child. I felt high on estrogen and self-righteousness, like an alley cat picking a fight with a puffed up tail.

The first person I'd told, beyond my immediate circle of friends, was my department chair, in a conversation that had me feeling like a little girl confessing she'd done something horribly wrong. I thought of my skittish cat, slinking across the apartment with her ears low. It wasn't the mood I'd intended to set.

"I have something to tell you," I said, when I sat down in the extra chair his office, aware that my tank top and shorts were much too tight. His hands, I noticed, were folded on his lap. Mine were clammy and shaking. He kept a yoga mat and a small refrigerator in his office; framed pictures of his grandchildren covered the flat surfaces and hung on the walls. Sometimes I thought if I were ever an administrator I would want to be like him. His presence was calming. "Well, I'm not sure how to say this, so here goes. I need to take a leave of absence in the spring."

His brows furrowed. "Is everything okay?"

"Yes. Oh, yes." Nothing about the conversation was going how it went in my head. "It's just, well, I'm expecting a baby in February."

"Oh. Oh. This is good news?" It seemed like a funny thing to ask, but I'm sure this was the last thing he'd expected me to say.

"Oh, yeah. Yeah. I'm really happy about it." I vaguely wondered why I didn't sound convincing. The progesterone kept me floating on a cloud. In the end, all my I'm-having-a-baby conversations were comical and touching.

Grayson, another one of my senior colleagues—a kind, soft-spoken man who always carried a topless mug of coffee and a thick paperback when he walked across campus—upon learning I was taking time off, knocked tentatively at my office door and hovered, before he finally asked me if I had cancer. I guess I'd hidden the baby lust and the insanity of fertility treatment pretty well my first two years on campus. I finally felt like they were getting to know me, not just the scholar who wrote articles on loss in twentieth-century literature or the teacher of poetry, but a young woman with desires that couldn't be contained in a library or a classroom with stained-glass windows. What they whispered to each other behind the closed doors of their offices or wrote in emails

I will never know, but outwardly I was met with nothing but acceptance. I wore pink dresses when I taught gender studies and answered questions for the school paper on the new maternity leave policy. My students clapped when I told them I was pregnant. Some days, when the light hit the birds standing defiantly on the telephone wires, I imagined I could live in Texas forever.

I wheeled my suitcase across the baggage claim at Newark, looking for my family. I found them on plastic chairs, both my siblings on their cell phones and my mother reading Oprah's magazine.

My sister smiled and hung up when she saw me. "Go get your pregnant sister's suitcase," she ordered our younger brother.

"How are you?" she cooed, inspecting the bump. I wasn't sure if she was talking to me or her niece-or-nephew in progress.

"Fine," I said, speaking for my offspring.

"You look good," Mom said, giving me a quick squeeze.

Their hands were everywhere.

The last time I'd been here was a year ago, for my grandfather's funeral, in the midst of what Aimee had called the "fertility nonsense." We were back in Jersey this time for the unveiling of the tombstone. The unveiling of my pregnancy was a necessary fact as well. It was hard to hide; I'd been wearing maternity pants and oversized shirts for weeks.

I wondered which of the relatives my mother had told. My mom and sister had been with first people with whom I'd shared the Baby Plan, back when it was only as tangible as the parenting magazines on my coffee table. I'd taken it for granted that they'd be supportive. My mother's first comment was "I'm not surprised," and the only real question she asked was "Why now?" My sister couldn't have been more thrilled. She coveted children in her own way, teaching special education. I wasn't embarrassed or ashamed—after all, I'd decided to get pregnant with more thought and deliberation than many couples. I had a job. I had money in the bank. But I wasn't sure I wanted my sex life (or lack thereof) to be up for discussion at Sunday brunch.

We stayed, for the last time, in my grandparents' home. The life that they'd created together was being dissembled piece by piece. The large upholstered sectional that covered two walls in the living room looked wan from lack of use; the kitchen table was gone (my cousin, I think, had taken it to his new house in Vermont); and the bed, with a head indention on the pillow, looked like something out of Faulkner. A year after his death, my grandfather's pills lined up in the medicine chest in the bathroom, an old TV guide sat on the side table in the den. The refrigerator was completely bare, and the cupboards had been emptied, their contents taken to local food banks. We bought supplies for breakfast at the Shop Rite down the street and ate dinner at an Italian restaurant close by. The whole thing wigged me out.

I thought about all the meals we had once shared as a family, meals when my grandfather and his brother haggled over who would pay the bill. And I thought about my grandfather's generation dying off and the baby squiggling in my uterus and my cousins' infants and toddlers. Whatever I believed about choosing family, my own body threatened to betray. Family was born, and I took my place in a line of Jewish women, ready to pass on blessings and matzoh ball recipes to the next generation. I thought about my mother being my age, and her father being her age, and I was saddened by the enormity of it all. I didn't want her to get old.

The next morning, my mother drove the rental car through the winding streets of New Brunswick, past the apartment where she'd locked herself in the bathroom at age three and kept a chicken in their basement storage area, past her elementary school and the park where she'd ice-skated all winter, and parked the car at the golf course across the street from the old Jewish cemetery. I figured it was only a matter of time before the golf course wanted to expand and they'd get some paperwork from the city to have the graves moved. My grandmother and grandfather were buried here, and there was another cemetery across town where the great-grandparents rested. My mother made an annual trip to visit all the dead relatives around the high holy days. Their graves mapped her hometown. Someday, I knew, I'd take the trip with her, pointing them out to my own son or daughter. Family encircled me.

While we waited for the Rabbi, we collected stones to place on top of the granite slab. Walking up and down the grassy area by the fence, I scavenged for one that wasn't too small and one that wasn't too big, not something that looked like chipped concrete but something more like marble. I wandered through the rows looking at names and dates. Some of the dead were children; I pictured brown-haired girls shivering on a boat from the old country and then dying in the influenza epidemic, alone in a small bedroom while their parents worked in the shirt-waist factory. My uterus clenched around the baby, busy doing back flips, and held her close.

Slowly the other relatives arrived, my aunt and uncle and cousin in his big SUV, my mother's cousins, my grandma's sister Mary and my grandfather's brother Henry, who had managed to outlive all their siblings. This mismatched pair was the closest I had to grandparents left. In Sunday school, we'd done family trees before our sophomore year confirmation class. I'd dutifully called relatives on the phone, wrote down their stories. The project was probably in a box in my mother's basement somewhere. I felt like the bearer of history. I didn't want to lose it. What stories would I have when my son asked? One half of his family tree was already chopped down.

I found my mother's first cousin walking with his son, who was young enough to be my child. I'd always liked his family. For my Bat Mitzvah, almost two decades ago, they'd given me a copy of the complete Shakespeare, its pages edged with gold. While everyone piled corned beef and rye bread on their plates in the dining room, I held their older son, Benjamin, on my lap. He'd suffered some kind of birth injury no one really talked about and ended up permanently brain damaged. He had CP and couldn't really see or hear and spent his life in a wheelchair, with a feeding tube. I hadn't gone to his funeral—that had been in the midst of The Bad Year—but in my heart I named my firstborn for him.

"So, how's Texas?" he asked. "I was looking on a map, trying to see where you are. That's just a huge state, isn't it?"

I squinted to look up at him. The sun was too bright for a trip to the cemetery. "Yeah, it might as well be its own country," I said. "Texas is fine."

"You like the school?"

"I do. I mean, it's a great job. I have good colleagues, interesting students. It's just...Texas. It's September and it's still ninety degrees there, you know?"

"I know your mother would like to have you closer to home."

"Me too."

"So what else is going on?"

That seemed like as good an opportunity as any to try out my news. "Well," I said, "I'm pregnant." I smoothed down the front of my shirt as a visual aid.

"Oh," I think he said, "congratulations." "Who's the father?" he continued, without missing a beat.

I supposed it was a natural, albeit intrusive, question to ask. After all, most people who get pregnant are at the very least dating the father-to-be, and the last time I'd shown up at a family gathering with a date was my brother's Bar Mitzvah, right before I headed off to graduate school. But it also struck me as one of those questions that says at least as much about the questioner as the questionee. For me, the father was the least important part of the story, only necessary for about a split second when sperm met egg.

I figured a blunt question demanded a blunt response. I shrugged and smiled a coy little smile. "Sperm donor," I said, and walked away, joining my mother by the gravesite. I put my chin on her shoulder, claiming my place.

Our cousin the rabbi said blessings over the grave. We set our stones on the tomb, Sam and Anne, husband and wife, beloved parents and grandparents. My child, boy or girl, would be named for them.

Afterward, we had lunch at a hotel downtown, a cluster of round tables, a chorus of hushed conversations, some of which, I assumed, were about me.

My aunt, who once bathed me and pinned up my hair, who took me to Spain and offered me sips of sangria at a tapas bar when I was seventeen, gave me a copy of a parenting book by a renowned expert. Or, at least he'd been a renowned expert decades ago. I took it home with me and put it proudly next to my growing library of books on child development and attachment parenting. I figured this was as close to acceptance as I'd ever get.

5.

MY UNDERWEAR WAS WET. My students were watching a film, and I kept getting up to go to the bathroom. I'd feel a rush of fluid and then a damp spot on my underwear. This had been happening for a couple days, since the trip to New Jersey. And now I was starting to panic. I read an article online that said in cases of premature rupture of membranes onset of labor generally occurred within the week. And at one day shy of seventeen weeks, I knew what that meant. No baby. Again.

After class, I sat through a seemingly endless committee meeting, feeling the baby sloshing around, my abdomen tensing periodically with what I hadn't yet figured out were contractions. I went home. I changed my underwear. I tried to reassure myself; it was so hot at school, I might just be really sweaty. I changed my underwear, I sat on the couch, and there it was again, a quick gush of fluid. This wasn't a time for second-guessing or embarrassment. I called the after hours number of the obstetrician's office and explained the situation to person from the answering service.

The on-call doctor called me back almost immediately. "Robin? This is Dr. Banks. Tell me what's going on."

"I keep feeling this fluid leaking. I really don't think it's urine."

"Is it clear?"

"Yes."

"Is it running down your leg?"

"No."

"Are you having contractions?"

"I'm not sure. I mean, I don't think so."

"I'd like you to lie down for a while and then get up. If it happens when you stand up, you need to come in to the hospital. Or, if you'd rather, I'm here for another couple hours, you can come in and get checked over. Either way."

I didn't give my answer any thought. "I'm really worried. I think I'd feel more comfortable having this looked at."

She gave me directions to the Labor and Delivery unit, which was in the hospital connected by a skyway to the building that housed her office. I'd never been inside before. I hadn't really wanted it to be a destination for another twenty weeks or so.

I changed out of my work clothes, into sweatpants and a T-shirt. There was a baby cricket chirruping in the bathtub. I couldn't bring myself to scoop him up and toss him out into the night. He hopped around, splashing in the remains of my morning shower. The sun was just beginning to go down. I couldn't face another hour down the highway by myself. I called Nona, who was so congested from a head cold that she sounded like one of her Spanish-speaking neighbors when she answered the phone. "Tell me when we're in the car," she said, when I started going into the story, "I'll be there in five minutes."

For most of the drive, we sat together in a thick silence. We passed all the usual sights, the Starbucks, the church with the big cross, the oil rig set against the orange sunset. Usually when we drove down the highway we played bad eighties pop tunes, Erasure or Depeche Mode. Tonight the only music was a symphony of sniffles and sighs.

When I imagined making this drive with Nona, I imagined it much later in the year, in labor during a February snow storm, me panting out the pains and Nona trying to drive fast enough to get us there but not fast enough to get a ticket, though sometimes, I thought she really did want us to get stopped by a cop and then escorted the rest of the way to the hospital. I had a sneaking suspicion. But maybe we'd never get that far. Maybe, tonight, this was it. I had a bad feeling, like the day I'd learned my first pregnancy wasn't viable. I couldn't go through that again. Not now. Not with a baby I could feel moving around.

Nona left me off at the entrance to the emergency room and went to park her car. "Can you tell me how to get to Labor and Delivery?" I asked someone with a nametag at the information desk. I followed the signs down the hall from the elevator, past the Neonatal Intensive Care Unit and the Cardiac Wing. I explained my situation at the nurses' station.

"Right. The doctor's expecting you. Let's get you in a room."

There was a baby warmer next to the bed. In the next room I could hear a woman grunting, and I thought she will push that baby through her body and the nurse will take him from her and place him here, with his cord clamped, to clean him up and hand him back, bundled, and she will put him to her breast. And I thought, if that doesn't happen they will take him and run him down the hall to the NICU, or the NICU team would come here, and I thought of all those awful episodes of *ER* I had watched where they intubated newborn babies who couldn't breathe on their own. I felt sick.

"Hey." Nona popped her head in to the room.

"Hey. Help me tie this gown?" They'd given me a hospital gown big enough to hold a woman the day she delivered and here I was, with this tiny bump. In any other circumstances, it would have been funny.

I don't remember telling her how scared I was, but I think I could see it in her eyes.

The nurse told me to get in bed and asked me about a thousand questions. When was my last period? What medications was I taking? When was the last time I'd eaten something? Who was my emergency contact?

Thankfully, the doctor knocked on the door. "Hi, I'm Dr. Banks," she said. She was one of Dr. Black's partners, another native Texan with long blonde hair. "Why don't we get you checked out."

"Okay." I settled back into the bed while a nurse fiddled with a monitor. It was like a blood pressure cuff for the abdomen, with discs that resembled hockey pucks. She wiggled the hockey puck around until she found the baby's heartbeat, twice as fast as mine.

"That sounds great," the doctor said. "Baby's clearly not in any distress."

"That's the heart?" Nona asked.

I nodded. I listened to it almost every night on a doppler I'd rented online, moving it slowly over the slope of my belly. Usually it picked up two heartbeats, my own blood chugging through the placenta and the fast gallop of the child swimming around my uterus. It was my lullaby and bedtime story. It still made me want to cry.

"Have you had more fluid leaking since you called?" the doctor asked.

"Yeah, a little." I folded my hands under my head—I wasn't sure where else to put them, with my abdomen tied up and exposed.

She asked to see the pad I'd been wearing. I blushed. That was pretty awkward, even for a gynecologist. "It's on the chair," I said, "folded up with my clothes.

The doctor inspected my underwear, her gloved hand going over the wet spot like they do in commercials for feminine hygiene products to prove how well they keep you dry. She was so serious and intent on her work that it was hard to stay embarrassed. She sighed a good sigh.

"Now this isn't typically what we see in patients who have ruptured their membranes."

"So I came in for nothing." I felt stupid for wasting her time, for dragging Nona away from her books and her bowl of chicken soup. It was a school night.

"Well, no, it's possible there is a high, slow leak. And it's always better to be safe than sorry. Your chart says you have APA? Have you been taking your shots?"

"Yeah, in fact I should be doing one about now."

"Well, let's take a peek and hopefully you can be on your way home."

They positioned me in the bed with my feet in stirrups and I looked at the baby warmer and I wanted to pass out.

"Relax, Robin. Let's check out this baby, okay? Press on her fundus?" she said to the nurse.

And the nurse put her hand at the top of the bump and pressed down hard, while the doctor put a piece litmus paper up against my cervix. If it turned a certain color, that meant I was leaking amniotic fluid. "Press again," she instructed the nurse. "Now, Robin, I want you to push."

That wasn't what I wanted to hear.

"It's okay. Your cervix isn't dilated at all. Now push." She said it gently, and I thought of all the babies she had delivered, telling their mothers that exact word. I supposed it was one of the most important verbs in all of human existence.

"Everything looks okay," she said, snapping off her gloves and dropping them in the wastebasket near the bed. "So we're going to let you go home. When are you supposed to see Dr. Black?"

"Not for a few weeks. I just saw her last Friday."

"Keep your scheduled appointment, but call if this keeps happening. It's good you came in. This is the kind of emergency visit I like. Just take it easy this weekend. Trust your body."

Taking the doctor's advice wasn't a hardship. I caught Nona's cold and spent the weekend in bed with a box of Kleenex and a mug of green tea. I read and re-read the paperwork from the hospital, the symptoms to watch for, reasons to call the doctor or head straight to the E.R. I wasn't bleeding. I wasn't having regular contractions. I wasn't gushing liquid every time I sat up or walked. Still, it was there, what seemed like a steady trickle and a niggling sense that something wasn't right. I didn't know what to do. I thought of my little cat Dannon, drowning in her saliva and refusing to eat, how I'd driven her to the vet who said there was nothing really wrong, just a behavioral problem. By the time they x-rayed her chest the next day, it was too late to help her. She died alone in an oxygen cage. I wouldn't let that happen again.

First thing Monday morning, I called my OB, who told me to come in for a sonogram that afternoon to check on fluid levels.

I lay on the table in the sonogram room. The sonographer spread thick blue gel across my belly and adjusted the bed so I could get a better look. It was the first time I'd had a sonogram without the probe. She moved the transducer back and forth across my skin, and there was a picture of a child's spine, its skull, its waving arms and legs. The baby kicked wildly. I stared out the profile of the face, the pointed little nose and the indentation of the lips.

"Did you feel that?" the technician asked. "This baby looks like it's running a race."

I nodded.

"Do you want to know the gender?"

"If you can tell. I mean, I don't want to find out later if it's something other than what you think it is. But if you know for sure."

"I'm never wrong," she said confidently.

"Okay then."

"Well, this baby is a girl." She wiggled the wand around again and got a nice shot of what she said was the kid's rear end. "See these two lines? Those are labia."

"Wow." I was having a girl.

The sonographer drew a bow on her head. I think I was suitably appalled.

She will be wrapped in pink blankets. She will wear ribbons in her hair and eyelet dresses. She will wear pigtails and ask for a pony for her birthday. She will play with dolls dressed in her old clothes, pastel sweaters and booties trimmed with lace. She will bake cookies in a play oven and share them with teddy bears for tea. She will sit with her legs crossed. She will wear pink lipstick and eye shadows that glint in the sun. She will learn to say no.

"I not a baby. You till my baby," she will say to me, kissing me on the side of the head.

"That's right," I smile. "You're not a baby, but you'll always be my baby."

"I a big gril."

"Yes, you are a big girl."

"I go at Monkey Room when I bigger."

"Yes, you can go to the Monkey Room when you are two and a half. That's very soon."

"I play baseball when I bigger?"

"Sure, honey, you can play baseball when you get bigger. What else do you want to do?"

"Ummmm, I dunno."

"Are there other games you want to play?"

"I play baseball. And soccer ball. And game with big stick."

"You want to play field hockey?"

"I like hockey! Yay!" She shakes her fists in the air, a miniature cheerleader with pompons.

"Yeah, hockey's a really fun game. I bet Grandma would teach you how to play hockey."

"Grammy like hockey too, Mom?"

"Grammy likes all kinds of games. Grammy teaches kids how to play sport games."

"Grammy a teacher? You a teacher too, Mom? I go at your work last night. I go pick you up with Gram."

"Yes, honey, Mommy is a teacher. And that's right, you did pick me up at work the other day."

"Last night."

"Right, the other day."

"You a gril, Mom?"

"Yes, sweetie, I'm a girl."

"I a gril too! Yay!"

I am in the thick of girl. I have a maternity dress, soft, with red paisleys that look like uteruses up and down the fabric. My face is round, my hair curls wild.

I do not believe in biological determinism. I do not believe that women are born to have children. But I have never been so entrenched in my body, my own sex, my uterus eclipsing the rest of my organs, heavier each day. I have never been more woman, and I am growing a girl.

6.

NONA AND I CAME UP WITH A PLAN to pretend we were a lesbian couple, should anyone be inclined to ask. We were back on the highway, driving to the first of our prepared childbirth classes, now that I'd finally made the decision to have her in the room with me for the birth. That was one of the small plot details in the narrative of becoming a single mother that I'd found most difficult to pin down. My mother was in some ways the most logical choice, having been through this whole ordeal three times, but she lived halfway across the country, and I wasn't sure the baby would be willing to accommodate her grandmother's work schedule. Likewise, I could imagine my sister putting on blue scrubs and rubbing my back for hours upon hours, but only if the baby agreed to be born on a prescheduled date and if the hospital had free WiFi. So that meant having someone local in the room with me, which, in practical terms, meant either Nona or Cara, colleagues and comrades, who'd already escorted me more times than I cared to count down this long, winding, often bumpy road (and, no, that's not a metaphor).

I was wearing my old yoga pants, ironically purchased from the children's department, pulled down under the belly, and an oversized sweatshirt I'd filched from Dr. Boy. Nona wore her signature flannel and jeans. We both pulled our hair back in ponytails. In the back of the car rested a stack of blankets and pillows I thought to grab before she picked me up.

I had a pretty good idea of what to expect, based on all

those silly images in TV sitcoms with women panting "hoo-hoo-hoo." But this pregnancy was less romantic comedy than feminist utopia. There would be no hoo-hooing for me. Nona concurred. When I imagined my labor, lying in the bathtub reading *The Thinking Woman's Guide to a Better Birth*, I imagined adopting various yoga poses, soft music in the background. The picture I'd conjured up felt like a homebirth with a midwife, not labor at a state-of-the-art medical center. The real reason I'd signed us up for the class, other than acquainting Nona with the ins and outs of my uterus, was to reconcile the ideal with the plausible. High risk pregnancies and homebirths really didn't mix.

Still, I don't think either of us was expecting a skinny blonde who looked like she taught aerobics in her spare time to be our childbirth educator. We were late; we made our way to the back of the room just in time for her to shove the podium out of the way and hop up on the long table to demonstrate how to contort our heavily pregnant bodies into supposedly comfortable positions.

I looked at Nona and rolled my eyes. The baby turned a somersault in agreement.

"Let's just think about this as anthropology," I think she said.

"Yeah, that's how I approach faculty meetings in the chapel." Admittedly, that was one of the most disconcerting aspects of life at the College. I felt just as out of place now as I did at meetings that began with prayers to make us better teachers and scholars.

From our seats in the back row, it was easy to survey the room. Sitting next to us was another girl-girl team; the pregnant one was in a turtleneck and overalls that drew attention to the shape of her belly. Everyone else was an obvious hetero couple; many of the men put rubbed the women's backs or rested hands possessively on an arm or thigh. It might as well have been a video on mating practices in animal kingdoms; I could almost smell the testosterone thick in the room.

Next the Blonde showed us a video of a woman getting an epidural. I shifted restlessly, trying to find a position that didn't hurt, and took a swig of water. Around us, the women in their floral maternity shirts sat back comfortably in their chairs and rubbed their bellies, attentively watching the screens. Apparently almost everyone who gave birth at this hospital had an induced labor and an epidural. I didn't want either one. After the D&C, I'd had enough of numbed toes to last me a lifetime, and the pain relief had been questionable at best.

"No way in hell," Nona said when the film was over. She put her hand protectively on her own stomach. The couples around us whispered in each other's ears.

"I think I'm going to hurl." The woman in the movie sat on the bed in the birth room, blissfully unaware that she was having contractions, though the monitor and everyone else in the room told her she was. The scene was as eerie as a B-movie.

It was good to know Nona and I were on the same page.

When it was time for break, we followed the rest of the pregnant couples to the vending machine upstairs for water and soft drinks. In the elevator, we swapped notes about due dates and doctors.

"Oh, yeah, we're using Dr. Black too. She's really fabulous," one of the dads said.

"Oh, yeah," I smiled. Fabulous if you want an induction and an epidural or a bikini wax. Lately she'd had a sign on her office door advertising skin care products and spa treatments. While she was incredibly aggressive when it came to medical care, she was also pretty enough that she could have won a statewide beauty contest in her youth. She certainly knew her clientele.

"I'll meet you back in the room," I told Nona, ducking into the bathroom along with all the other pregnant people. Nona hung with the dads. They bonded over the goodies they got to have while their partners labored—crackers and juice in the nurse's station—not just a never-ending supply of orange popsicles.

When we reconvened, the Blonde rattled off our other options for pain management, as she called it. Apparently there was a drug that made you feel like you'd had a margarita.

"Can I get one?" one of the dads said. I didn't get the sense that he was joking.

"Can I just say I am so happy I don't have one of those?" I said to Nona. When I'd signed up for the class I thought maybe I'd be envious, seeing all those doting fathers-to-be giving their wives little kisses and stolen glances. But, really, when I looked around the room, I couldn't imagine myself sitting there with Dr. Boy or any of the other boyfriends I'd had through the years. When it came down to it, I had no desire to share the pregnancy with anyone; this baby was all mine. I'd found myself when that second line came up on the pee stick.

"Is anyone here planning on doing a natural birth?" the Blonde asked.

I was the only one who raised my hand.

"I got all the way to eight centimeters," the Blonde said, obviously very pleased with herself, "and I just couldn't take it anymore. But the nurses here are very supportive of women who want to try without medication."

Of course, the Blonde wasn't really giving us much in the way of useful information about how to keep ourselves calm enough to make it through labor without the margarita drug.

"Are we going to talk about C-sections?" an anxious woman blurted out, almost in tears. "My baby is breech and the doctor said I need to have a C-section."

"Of course," the Blonde said, in a soothing mommy voice. "Everyone here needs to be prepared. Most C-sections are not planned. We'll talk about that in our last class, okay? Now who's ready for a good back rub?"

On the floor on our nest of pillows and blankets, Nona worked the kinks out of my shoulders and lower back. It was the most delicious thing I'd felt in months, and all I needed to do was take her to dinner. But I wouldn't have traded single pregnancy for anything, not even a live-in masseuse.

The night of our last class I kept staring at the clock while the Blonde yammered on and on about how it was a bad idea to put balloons in the yard to welcome the new mother home, as it told prospective kidnappers there was a new baby on the block. Our babies, she assured us, would be protected with a LoJack attached to their heels for electronic monitoring in post-natal wards.

The last hour we would head over to the hospital to get a tour, coo at some fresh-from-the-womb kiddos at the nursery and meet with some of the L&D nurses. I wondered if I should check myself in. I'd been having contractions since before Nona and I got in the car for the drive, and they weren't stopping. Maybe this was it. I'd been preparing myself for The Bad Thing for months. It was strange. I was the happiest I'd ever been, lured into complacency by a hormonal fog. But in the pit of my stomach was the old fear. I wasn't on bed rest or medication for preterm labor. The baby was healthy, growing steadily—I had a series of sonogram images to prove it. But there it was, every time I made an appointment, *high risk*, every time I took a shot of heparin, every time I had a non-stress test to check the baby's heart. I couldn't bring myself to buy a crib. In the end, I wasn't sure I'd get to bring a baby home, the baby I'd wanted for more than three years.

On the walk over to the hospital I lagged behind everyone else, my belly a clenched fist. I was born at thirty-three weeks, and here I was, now, just under thirty-two weeks along. The first day of class they had said to us they now resuscitate babies born at twenty-four weeks and weighing one pound. At twenty-three weeks and fifteen ounces you probably have a second-trimester miscarriage; an ounce and a day later you're a mom to a preemie who could probably look forward to poor eyesight, developmental delays, and a lifetime of medical problems, should she survive the birth. The line blurred into fog.

I leaned against the wall in the labor room. We'd been here before, Nona and I, and if we stayed here tonight I would have a child who would, in all likelihood, live. I went through the statistics in my head. She'd be small and would probably need to stay on a respirator in the NICU for weeks; I thought of the pictures in my album at home, my mother wearing a hospital gown and mask while she fed me with a small glass bottle every day for more than a month. It seemed like the only possible ending to this story.

Behind the nursery glass there was a man taking pictures of a newborn in an incubator, two sets of footprints inked on his blue hospital vest.

"That one's a C-section," the Blonde said, knowingly. "Twins. See? There are two sets of footprints on the Dad's shirt, and he's got a mask on."

Nona was excited about the Dad Shirt she'd get to take home. I saw the glint in her eye. She loved to paint. I could see her making a stencil of the baby's foot and using it instead of wallpaper to decorate the room. To be fair, I had a thing for baby feet, too. The collection of tiny socks in my drawer was growing steadily.

"Well, that's it, folks," the Blonde said. "I will probably see some of you back here in a few weeks. And don't forget to sign up for your infant CPR courses. They're held in the room around the hall, across from the NICU."

I felt sick. There were chairs in a lobby area where the one walkway met another walkway to go across to the professional building. We sat for a while, listening to the hum of the vending machines. I wanted someone to tell me what to do.

"We can go back, if you think we need to go back," Nona said.

"I think it's okay." The contractions weren't stopping, but they weren't getting any closer together either, which was what everyone said happened during actual labor. I didn't want to spend the night in the hospital for another false alarm. I didn't want to end up on drugs for preterm labor.

"We can get you checked out if you're worried."

"No, it's okay." I wished there was a manual on what to do in situations like this. It was never as cut and dried as the doctors made it sound.

We made it out to the car, eventually. These days I had about ten good steps before I felt like collapsing. I'd gained about thirty pounds already. My hips and thighs and lower back ached all the time. Why didn't they ever tell you pregnancy made it hard to walk? TV shows always made fun of women wobbling and waddling but, jeez, it hurt. The pain went deep into my bones.

Nona drove us home in my car, while I kept my hand on my belly and breathed. On the radio, Sheryl Crow was singing "The First Cut is the Deepest." The baby wiggled around, and I cried, willing her to stay put.

7.

THAT WEEKEND, my mother came for a visit, suitcases loaded with hand-me-down baby clothes for me and a vacation supply of chocolate, thanks to the goodness of her fifth graders, for her. It was the first time she'd been back to Texas since she helped me move in more than two years ago, but less than two months from my due date there was no way I was getting on a plane to go home for winter break. So I drove to pick her up at the airport, following a sequence of roads so familiar I had to remind myself to turn right at the exit for the airport, instead of continuing on to the clinic. It was warm—warm enough to skip a winter coat altogether—and I thought about all those years my grandparents met us at gate for winter trips to Florida, stripping off layers of sweaters as we navigated ourselves through the airport and out to the car, parked in the shade of a palm tree. Texas wasn't nearly as tropical, but it certainly didn't make for white Christmases, which I very much liked, even though Christmas wasn't a holiday I celebrated. My menorah sat in a box in the back closet; I'd used the candles for a makeshift lantern the last time the power went out. Maybe next year I'd spray my windows with snowy patterns, fry up some latkes, and read the Hanukkah story to the baby.

I managed to find a parking space that was right across from baggage claim, for which I was extremely grateful, as my hips ached so much from the drive that I could barely make it across the street. I'd been back and forth on the long highway three days in a row—enough time in the car to make it halfway back to Indiana. It felt like the good old days of fertility treatment. Yesterday, when the contractions were still coming steadily, Nona had driven me back to the hospital to get checked over by Dr. Banks; she hooked me up to a monitor for half an hour, decided she didn't see anything too alarming, and sent me on my way with a promise to drink a lot of water and lie on my left side. Something about dehydration causing muscle cramps and a large blood vessel that functioned better in that position.

Mom was waiting for me by the time I walked past the vending machines and checked the monitors to see if her plane had arrived. "Wow, you're huge!" she said by way of greeting. Mom wasn't one to mince her words.

I was pretty enamored with my girth but couldn't resist the opportunity to correct her. "Actually, the nurses at the doctor's office always talk about how small my belly is compared to the other patients."

She shrugged. "Whatever." She managed to get her arms around me for a hug, despite the purported enormity of my waistline. I actually wondered if, by the end, I'd fit behind the steering wheel of my car.

We walked out to the car, Mom pulling her suitcase while I carried a tote bag full of magazines and extra candy bars. "Are you hungry?" I asked, popping open the trunk to stash her bags. "I thought we could stop in town to get something to eat and go over to the Babies 'R' Us to look at the strollers and cribs. Nona keeps yelling at me because I don't have any of the required stuff yet."

Jewish women weren't supposed to have baby showers, my mother insisted. And while I wouldn't consider myself a practicing Jew, this was one time I didn't want to tempt fate. Preparation was one thing; celebrating a child who wasn't yet born seemed quite another, especially when the doctor took every available opportunity to remind me the pregnancy was high risk. "It's good you came in," Dr. Banks had said. "We need to watch this pretty closely."

"Sure. You want me to drive?"

I smiled my Texas smile. Even though I was a thirty-year-old mother-to-be, it was really nice having my own mom around.

We spent the week of her visit going back and forth to the city, alternating tourist attractions and shopping trips with afternoons in the movie theater. The pace was delightful. I'd gone straight from college to graduate school to a tenure track job; usually I spent winter break preparing for spring courses, not lounging around with the TV on. At night she'd cook roast beef or baked chicken or whatever else I fancied while I soaked my foot in a stockpot filled with hot water and Epsom salts, as I'd managed to acquire an ingrown toenail after my very first pedicure, which was a birthday present from Lynn. A month later, all my other toes still looked polished and pretty against the puffy white of my swollen feet. Mom seemed to get some kind of perverse pleasure out of "cooking my foot," as we referred to her science project, and I was certainly happy to oblige her with sitting on the couch with the television on. Even if the doctor decided to induce labor early, something I hadn't really wanted to ask about, I still had five or six weeks to go.

"So I liked that blue stroller," Mom announced from the kitchen, where she was doing the dishes, her hands coated with soap bubbles. A gym teacher by profession, she had a hard time sitting still; she was always scrubbing dishes and washing windows and watering plants until, finally, she collapsed on the couch and fell asleep with the TV in the background, a tendency she'd inherited from my grandmother that we referred to as the Kessler Sleeping Gene. I hoped it was one of those things that could skip a generation, as I was an insomniac from infancy, when I couldn't be bothered with an afternoon nap until, she'd told me, I collapsed in a heap on the kitchen floor.

She turned off the water and dried her hands with the dishtowel she kept on her shoulder, so it was always readily available. "But I'm not sure I believe that sales guy that you can really open and close it with one hand."

We'd just made our second trip to the Babies 'R' Us, where we pulled one stroller after another off the shelves and practiced opening and closing it and pushing it around the store. Most of them were enormous, designed for people about a foot taller than me. I'd pretty much decided on a blue and black checker print one, because it had good reviews and was not pink; it also happened to be the lightest model they carried, at a mere sixteen pounds.

"Have you told your father about the baby?" Mom certainly had a way with segues.

I fussed with the old afghan on my lap, smoothing it across my legs, as I deliberated over what to say. "No. I mean, I've thought about it, but I'm not sure what I want from him, you know?" There was a hole in the blanket, where a crocheted loop had come undone; I pushed my finger through it. My grandmother had tried to teach me to knit when I was seven; I made a scarf for my dolls while she watched *Days of Our Lives* on television. This white and tan one my mother had knitted, and I'd carted it from my dorm room in college to my apartment in Indiana to the back of my new sofa in Texas, one of a handful of objects in my apartment imbued with family history. "I mean, I haven't talked to him in, like, ten years or something. And I don't see the point in telling him anything unless I'd like to see him. And I'm not sure I do. Does that make sense?"

"Yes. But it might be nice to let him know he's going to be a grandfather."

My mother's loyalty to an ex-husband that she'd once sued for child support was one of her oddest and most endearing features. She'd always made a point not to talk badly about him, but I know she also secretly hoped that my sister and I would come to the same conclusions about him that she did. The truth was I imagined my baby's life would be much simpler without a father. Families were complicated enough without ex-husbands and step-parents.

"Well, he'll find out. He probably already knows. I told Grandma. And she said he would write me a letter or something."

She wiped her hands on the dishtowel and put it back on her shoulder; she surveyed the apartment, looking for another project to tackle. She resembled a cat, ears pulled back and ready to pounce on the next thing that moved. "And you haven't heard from him?"

"No, Mom, I haven't heard from him. Can you get me some more hot water for my foot, please?"

I pulled my foot out of the tepid water and dried it off, while Mom lugged the pot back into the kitchen, refilled it from the tap, and put it back on the stove to heat. We'd been having the same conversation about my father's family for years; my only contact with them was through my grandmother, whom I called largely out of a sense of guilt. She didn't understand me. She didn't understand why I wasn't talking to my father, and she didn't understand why I'd spent seven years pursuing a graduate degree in English literature (of all things) instead of looking for a husband. She never said this directly, but I could tell. When we talked, she asked about the boy I was dating, not the papers I was writing. I'd written many more papers than I'd been on dates. Finally, in the past few months, she had stopped talking about my father, asking me what went wrong between us, and urging me to call him.

To be honest, I wasn't sure that I could articulate the reason we weren't speaking in a way that meant sense to anybody else. I didn't hate him. He didn't abuse me or do anything that struck me as horribly wrong, except for not paying child support, which, to be fair, hadn't affected my life in any appreciable way; it was the symbolism I resented. But he hadn't done anything right either. The sum total of my memories of him during my childhood were of him sitting on the couch watching a ball game while my sister and I played Star Wars action figures or ran around the block with our stepbrother, and then him driving us home in his smoke-filled Volkswagen, at which point my stepfather would sit me down on the basement couch to talk. Eventually, bearing a handful of used Kleenex and puffy red eyes, I would go upstairs to my room and read my latest acquisition from the library, hating both men I called Dad. In high school, I resented the weekends I gave up hanging out with my friends so I could visit my father, coming home in a coat that always reeked of cigarette smoke. I had a special denim jacket I reserved for seeing him; he bought it for me in junior high school, and I wore it for years, until it was faded and too small, and he never asked me why my mother didn't buy me a new coat. His method of parenting was taking us to movies and expensive dinners and buying us gifts, and even then, even when my stepfather was out of a job and we couldn't afford anything resembling a luxury, I knew I didn't want to be bought.

Now, well into my own adulthood, I'd been without a father so long I didn't feel like I was missing anything. I'm sure that if I went into therapy the shrink would say that my desire to be a single parent had to do with my inability to trust men, a father who'd had an affair and left my mother when I was four, a stepfather who was more like my mother's fourth child, throwing tantrums and refusing to help out around the house, than a real parent. And maybe that's right. But as the reality of becoming a single parent became clearer with each pound I gained, I was more certain than I'd ever been that I'd made the right choice.

Sure, sometimes, when I saw a pregnant woman with her husband, like the ones sitting in the rocking chairs at Babies 'R' Us, I had a quick pang of jealousy. After all, it would have been nice to have someone to fetch me the chocolate cake I craved at 9:00 at night, when I'd drag myself across town in a sweatshirt and pajama bottoms to scavenge for Little Debbies at the Piggly Wiggly, and it would have been nice to have someone rub my back at 3:00 in the morning when I woke because my hips hurt no matter what position I adopted. But those desires seemed petty and inconsequential. I'd noticed that I'd largely stopped daydreaming and making up stories in those quiet moments before bed; instead, I worried about lead paint and carbon monoxide poisoning and kidnappers at the park, the million things that could harm a child in the twenty-first century. And even then, I couldn't envision myself rolling over in bed to share my fears with a partner. I was alone, to be sure, but loneliness was far away as another country. I felt grounded, connected to my friends and the world.

By the time Mom left a week later, the second bedroom had been cleared out enough that I could see where I'd put a crib and a changing table and all the plastic contraptions that people having babies seem to require. The result of my nesting was a tower of cardboard boxes and a pile of papers I didn't know what to do with, shoved on top of the filing cabinet in the walk-in closet. Eventually, when I was able to lift things again, I'd take the work-related stuff to school. For now, I closed the door and ignored it.

After she left, I sat propped on my elbows on the twin bed, the only remaining piece of furniture in the room, and I tried to picture the baby and me in this space. I imagined myself in a rocker-glider with a newborn, moving back and forth slowly in the night, rubbing the soft skin on her arm or putting my pinkie finger in her mouth for her to suck. The scene was cozy and domestic, something from a TV show or mothering magazine. I placed her in the crib, gently, carefully, so she didn't wake up, and stood beside her, just watching her breathe, before closing her door and going into the kitchen to do dishes and tidy up and then settling on to the couch to relax. It was this kind of scene I'd once imagined when I thought of being a mother and I thought of it again now, my belly heavy with a daughter I couldn't quite see.

I knew her intimately, the curve of her bottom that arced outward from my ribcage, to her head wedged firmly in my pelvis. She wiggled back and forth, and I imagined her rolling in her sleep, trying to find a comfortable fit in this cradle of bones. I felt a tickle sometimes on the lower side of my belly, made by something smaller like hands or feet. I sat on the bed and caressed us both at the same time, breathing deeply, filling us and more fulfilled than I'd ever been. I was a woman who'd created her own fantasy—what could be better than that?

"The room is really coming together," Nona said, leaning heavily against the blue spindle crib that she and Sawyer had just assembled. The only thing I was good for was sitting on the bed and reading directions that couldn't have been more incomprehensible if they'd been in Swahili. The one thing I hadn't considered was how stupid pregnancy made me.

I looked around through her eyes at institutional beige walls and the crib, the ratty twin bed I was sitting on, and a plain white assemble-it-yourself bookcase that I'd bought in Indiana and put together with Dr. Boy's assistance. Thick corrugated cardboard that hadn't yet made it to the recycling center carpeted the floor, and a handful of toys and a stack of baby clothes sat in a laundry basket waiting for me to wash. It looked nothing like those cozy photos of sunlit nurseries in the catalogs.

I'd spent most of the previous night wrestling with the stroller, curled around wheels and handlebars and parent cup-holders, studying the instruction booklet and trying to knock the hard plastic into submission. The blue-shirted salesclerk had said it would take a mere thirty minutes to put together, but I supposed that was the estimate for agile young men who work the travel aisle at Babies 'R' Us, not enormously pregnant women. I'm not sure exactly why, but it was important to me to do this task myself, something like learning to drive in the city, that I needed to tackle before I could bring a baby home from the hospital and raise her on my own. Eventually, I managed to pop the wheels in place and figured out how to snap the infant seat into the stroller base. Then I strapped in one of the teddy bears from the growing pile in the baby's room and shoved it around the apartment. Pistachio ran for cover under the bed, tail and ears low to the ground, and after a few laps, I collapsed on the couch. Now the stroller sat next to the hall closet, awaiting its first trip with a real live baby.

In the soon-to-be nursery, Nona rifled through the basket of baby things and pulled out a blue and pink afghan that one of our colleague's wives had crocheted. She spread it neatly across the mattress, and tucked one of the bears in the corner. It looked cozy enough to climb into and go to sleep.

"Let's do the rocker," Sawyer said, ripping the oversized box, "and then let's get some of this cardboard out of here." Poor Sawyer had first gotten roped into lending his truck for the Great Baby Shopping Spree and now into assembling the furniture I'd brought home. I knew he'd rather be back at Nona's place working on his book, or hanging out with her. When I thought about the possibility of Nona living with him full time—she was always talking about applying for new jobs in faraway places that would let them live together instead of six hours apart—the reality tightened around me like a contraction.

"I really think you need to go back and buy that ottoman," Nona said, snapping the upholstered cushion to the rocker's oak frame. "Just think about it. You're sitting here with the baby and it's four in the morning and you have some place to put your feet up."

"I think you want the ottoman," I said, picturing her holding a newborn, her hair spilling out of a loose ponytail and slippered feet pushing off the footrest until she glided back and forth. She sang to the baby, quiet lullabies in a language that only the two of them shared. I couldn't tell if it was my baby or her baby that she was holding.

"I am partial to ottomans." She had a little footstool in her living room; she'd found it at a second hand store and covered it with bright squares of cloth. She put her feet there while she read for class, a fire in the fireplace and a glass of wine on the table beside her.

"I'll think about it. That way when you come over at four in the morning you have some place to put your feet up." I smiled and she laughed softly. Truly, I wondered how many lonely nights I'd feel desperate enough for company to call. I wondered how alone I'd really be. Picking out furniture and making fun of prepared childbirth class was one thing, rocking a colicky baby or washing loads of laundry stained with spit up was another. My friends were generous, loving people, but, excited as they were about this baby's impending arrival, they hadn't signed on to be co-parents. I was a single mother by choice, or would be, as soon as my daughter took her first independent breath. It was the *choice* that had seemed vital to me when I marched into Dr. C's office two years ago; now it was the word *single*. *Sex and the City* said it all; the single girl is a delightful temporary stop on the way to romance, be it straight or gay. From assembling baby furniture to attending family functions, the world wasn't designed for going it alone.

8.

WHEN I HEARD THE KNOCK I'd been expecting, I hauled myself off the couch, where I sat folding clothes, and waddled to
the front door. Dr. Boy was standing there, all six feet of him,
in his crisp jeans and black shoes, the faded orange T-shirt I
loved. Just like old times.

"Hey," he said, pulling my head into his chest.

"Hey." Even eight months pregnant, I fit next to him like
we were two sculptures carved from the same stone. "I'm
starving," I said.

"Well, I guess you're eating for two. That's what they say,
right?"

This was our last pre-baby get-together. I was trying to
squeeze in grown-up dates with all of my Texas friends before
I took my vow of solitude and motherhood. Chastity seemed
likely, too, as I'd soon lack the time to shower, much less put
on lipstick and head out on the town.

I drove, pointing out the sites, my belly inching closer to
the steering wheel. In the back, the infant seat was strapped
in the shoulder harness but not yet anchored; it slid back and
forth when I turned corners. Taking it to the police station to
have it properly secured was one of the many tasks that filled
my before-the-baby to-do list, a list I found myself ignoring.
Writing a will was the biggest thing I couldn't manage to bring
myself to do. I wondered what that really meant. Dr. Boy flipped
through the CDs I kept in the console and put on Aimee Mann.
Hold my hand on take-off, she crooned.

We settled into our booth at IHOP, one of those innocuous places that could have been in Any Small Town, USA, all the churchgoers in their Sunday best waiting in the lobby, kids playing Game Boys and adults flipping through the *Times*. Usually Dr. Boy didn't talk to anyone on Sunday morning. It was one of his things—like always facing the door to the restaurant—that intrigued me about him. Sometimes, I thought that's what being in love meant—finding someone else's peculiar details endearing rather than annoying. But loving him hadn't ever been the problem.

"Look at you," he said, pouring himself a cup of coffee from a white plastic carafe. "When I met you, you were what, twenty-three years old and maybe ninety-five pounds?" There was something like nostalgia in his voice, his long fingers around his coffee cup, and I thought about that one morning in Indiana when I woke up in his bed and he went out to buy us coffee and bagels and we sat together not talking before I went home to feed my cats. He'd said once that I used the cats as an excuse not to stay, which I think was his excuse for not making it clear that he wanted me to stay. We made a bad couple, but sometimes, like now, I wondered what would have happened if we had actually tried to be a couple at the same time. He never talked about the other women he was seeing, though I knew he had to be seeing someone; before I'd gotten pregnant, his strategic omissions left me feeling like, even though we rarely saw each other, he was still mine. Now my belly sat heavily between us like the wall in Frost's poem we always taught. We were a long way from the lecture hall, where we shared a table and caffeine in the back row.

"So what are you going to call her?"

"Hannah, I think, after my grandmother. I'm still stuck on the middle name. Janell, maybe. Or Jane." I'd spent hours going through books of baby names, writing down possibilities (Hannah Jane Hannah Janell Hannah Elizabeth Sarah Anne Samara Jane Samara Josephine) until I finally circled back to the only name that was really a possibility. I'd known this child would be named Hannah from the time I dreamed her up.

He chortled. "Hannah Jane. That's like the ultimate Texas name."

I swallowed. "I'm thinking about Sadie too. My grandfather's name was Sam."

"Sadie Silbergleid." He nodded heartily, a toothy grin lighting up his face. "She could be a romance novelist." He tapped my forearm with his index finger.

"Yeah, exactly what I want her to be when she grows up." I rolled my eyes.

"I thought feminists believed women have the right to choose their own life paths." He'd used that line on me before.

"Give me a break."

He rested his hand on my forearm, rubbing it a little with his index finger. "I'm just saying…"

The waitress came by to take our order and we watched her watching us: black man and white woman, no rings on our fingers and my belly so big it bumped the edge of the table. The restaurant was full of all kinds of people, families with six kids in their Wal-Mart shoes, faculty couples with their *New York Times*, and college kids still in their date-night clothes heavy with smoke. Past the people in the vestibule, past the parking lot, the highway stretched a seemingly infinite line in each direction, one toward the city, toward the hospital, toward the Boy; the other toward Oklahoma and, eventually, home. If I'd stood in the parking lot and looked far against the horizon, I could have seen an oil rig, the one landmark that never failed to remind me where I was.

"Sometimes I wonder if I'll be stuck here forever," I said to him. Even my voice had taken on a Southern twang; sometimes, I heard myself call my students "y'all" and wondered when I'd picked that up. Cara kept saying she was going to buy the baby cowgirl boots and a little Stetson hat to wear home from the hospital.

"Well," he admitted, "you made a choice to have a kid. I'm not saying that's a bad thing. But it makes it more difficult to get another job. I mean, when are you going to write?"

"I know." I took a sip of orange juice. "And it's not like I hate it here. My colleagues are great. I enjoy my classes, my students. I have funding to travel. It's a good deal, all things considered, especially when I listen to you talk about what it's like at a big state school. But I have this list in my notebook I keep coming back to, a list of all the things I want in a place to live, in a job..."

"What things?"

"Oh, silly things mostly. Like I don't want to have to drive an hour to buy organic meat. We don't even get NPR here. I want a good public library, with a real children's room and more than one measly shelf for new books. I want a place with actual seasons—I don't even need to button my coat and it's freaking January, you know? And I want my daughter to be able to see her grandmother and her aunt and uncle and not be the only Jewish kid in her class."

He nodded, knowingly, as I spoke. "So you'll go on the market next year?"

I let out a huge breath I hadn't realized I was holding. "I suppose. September feels really soon, though, too soon. I'd need a better writing sample, new letters of rec. When I told my department chair I was pregnant he asked if I would be back and I told him yes."

"You weren't lying."

"No, I suppose not. I mean, I will be back for the year at least. And I probably won't get a job, not the kind of job I want."

I looked out the window at Texas and wondered what would happen if I spent the rest of my life here, Ford trucks and dead armadillos on side of the road, nothing but open sky on the horizon. Across the parking lot from the IHOP was an old K-Mart, closed down. It sat there waiting to be demolished. I wondered what would take its place, and I wondered what it would take for me to think of this place as a permanent home.

There was no question, I had friends. And as the baby had grown inside me, the college had come to feel like a big extended family. A couple of my former students had gotten together and made a fleece blanket, patterned with Winnie the Pooh characters and colored letter blocks; it was the sort of blanket I imagined her lugging around for years. And in one of her strangest moments of sincerity and goodwill, Karen had offered to rub my feet. I couldn't conjure up the scene without laughing, but I was touched by the offer nonetheless.

There was a quote that I liked from James Baldwin's *Giovanni's Room*, one of my favorite books to teach, that talked about home. "I ached abruptly, intolerably, with a longing to go home; not to that hotel, in one of the alleys of Paris, where the concierge barred the way with my unpaid bill; but home, home across the ocean, to things and people I knew and understood; to those things, those places, those people which I would always, helplessly, and in whatever bitterness of spirit, love above all else." What Texas had taught me is that there's more to feeling at home in a place than having friends and a good job. There was something in the air here, something in the way the land met the sky, that I couldn't claim as my own. If I had grown to appreciate small town Texas, I missed the Midwest with a ferocity I couldn't quite understand. I missed the long stretches of cornfields that lined the roads, and the way the air felt in September, just as summer turned to fall and colored leaves speckled the roads like brightly colored footprints. I missed winters so cold I stayed in my bed under a down comforter and hibernated with a stack of books and a cup of hot tea. I was happiest in Texas when it snowed. After three years here, with this baby squiggling in my belly, I was at peace. Still, I was tired of smiling.

"You know, she's going to have a Texas birth certificate," Dr. Boy said, gently.

"I know. It's funny. My mom always complains about how she got stuck in Illinois. She was only there for my father's job and then they got divorced. But she has three kids who were born in Chicago and all her friends live there and I think it's only now that her parents died that she doesn't talk about New Jersey as home anymore. I don't want to spend the next thirty years living in a place that's not right, just because I have a good job, you know."

"Plenty of people do."

"You talk about leaving all the time." I tried to imagine my life in Texas without him, and I couldn't do it. I couldn't quite imagine leaving him either. I knew we would never marry—I could barely get him to commit to breakfast—but still, we were bound by the state.

When he left me at home—a hug and quick peck on the forehead—I sat on the couch and folded baby clothes. I thought about my daughter growing up with a Texas drawl and cowboy boots, a Texas flag on a T-shirt. I thought about my grandmother, standing at the edge of her driveway as our car pulled away, the force of her embrace, like she was trying to get the impression of us etched permanently in her arms, before we left for the airport, back to the cornfields and tornado drills and deep dish pizza we called home. When the phone rang later that afternoon, it was my mother, calling to check in. How could I keep her grandchild from her? How could I raise my daughter in a place I couldn't call *mine*?

9.

I AM IMMOBILE on the table, my back propped at forty-five degrees, belly exposed and strapped, a double monitor picking up each heart beat, each contraction. The baby is heavy and still, like a watermelon waiting to be carved. I watch her heart on the monitor. I try to slow my breath. My blood pressure, when the nurse takes it, is higher than it was yesterday, higher than it was last week, higher than it's ever been. For the past thirty-five weeks, I have been waiting for something to go wrong.

During the test, I read to my daughter, poems by Adrienne Rich, hope she will respond to the sound of my voice. She doesn't kick, doesn't punch, doesn't roll. I might as well have a bowling ball strapped to my abdomen.

Dr. Black comes in, looks at the monitor and the long print-out, folding on the floor. I've been here for an hour, strapped to this machine and its graph paper. She clucks her tongue against the roof of her mouth. "Let's try to wake this sleepy baby up." She places her hands on my belly and jostles it/me/her, much harder than I would touch myself, like she's slapping sense into the unconscious. "I'll be back in twenty minutes. Use the call button if she falls off the monitor."

The baby is obstinate, motionless, her spine curved along the left side of my uterus, pelvis curved up under my rib cage, head tucked down on the right, the position she's been in for months. There's no place left for her to move.

"She moving anymore?" my doctor says when she comes back in.

"Not really."

This is the second time we've been monitored in two days. Yesterday, she did the same thing, and the doctor sent me home with instructions to call if the baby didn't start moving more. When I spoke to the nurse that morning, she told me to drink some juice and lie on my left side and count the number of times she kicked. But as soon as I settled myself on the couch, she called back to say that the doctor wanted me to come in immediately. I left Nona a message on her school voicemail and got in my car. How many times, I thought, how many times have I driven down this highway, paved with panic?

"Okay," my doctor's voice is calm, she's always calm, but there is an undertone of something I've never heard, caution or concern. She braces herself against whatever will come. "Here's what we're going to do. I'm going to call Labor and Delivery to get you a room. We'll monitor you there for a few more hours, and I might do a sonogram."

"And then what?"

"Depending on what she does in the next few hours, I might let you go home. Or, it might be time to call it quits."

"Meaning?"

"We induce labor today." I remember what she'd said to me months ago, the first time I was in her office. *In cases like these, it's best to get the baby out of a hostile environment.* "You're at thirty-seven weeks; that's considered full term. Her lungs should be mature. Your blood pressure's going up every visit. This could be an indication of placental insufficiency. It's not worth waiting around for something to go wrong."

Increased risk of stillbirth is what she'd said when I asked her, again, why she wanted to induce early, even though all the books said early inductions almost inevitably fail. I can't find my voice.

She scribbles something in my chart, taps her pen against the file. "What time did you take heparin?"

"Around nine. Why?"

"It should be out of your system if we need to do a C-section. Who's your pediatrician?"

"I don't have one. I mean, I have one lined up at home, but not one affiliated with this hospital."

"I'll have the nurse call the guys downstairs, see if they take your insurance."

Dr. Black unhooks the monitors and waits while I pull my shirt back down and climb off the table, her hand on my arm to steady me. I slip my feet, one at a time, into my shoes. My movements are slow, deliberate. It's all happening too fast. I want to stop, sit down, eat a fruit tart. If life happens in small moments, story happens in huge leaps. This is it, I recognize, the turning point, the aptly named *crisis* when there's no going back, when the outcome has already been determined, when the conflict must be taken to its inevitable and logical conclusion. If this were a story, I'd know what happens next. But this is my life.

As the doctor talks, preparing me for what is to come, a contraction hardens my abdomen; pain wraps around my back like a girdle and settles in my groin. It feels like I am moving under water, against the current; everything is muffled but the sound of my own heart, galloping. I feel it in my chest and deep in my pelvis, where the placenta pulses, fighting to keep my daughter alive.

The doctor is still talking, her hand on my back, ushering me into the hall, toward the door to the waiting room. She hands me a thick envelope. "Give this to the nurse in L&D. I was just getting all your paperwork in order. If you need to call someone to meet you at the hospital, you should do it before you head across the street."

Outside the skyway that leads to the hospital, I sit on a bench. Buried in my backpack is the cell phone that my mother insists I carry, for emergencies such as these. Nona picks up on the first ring.

"I'll be there in an hour," she says. Terror thickens the air of the hallway until I can barely breathe.

I can't bring myself to cross the threshold. I take the paperwork out of the envelope and look at the sheets one at a time, the record of my weight and blood pressure at every prenatal appointment since July, the baby's measurements at sonograms, the medications I am taking, my doctor's narrative of my questions and her answers. *Re-explained the necessity of induction* she had written about my last appointment.

At home, my hospital bag sits open on my desk with a couple books inside but nothing else. No receiving blankets. No pajamas or nursing bras. I have not been able to bring myself to pack. I still haven't gone to the police station to get the car seat installed. I still haven't made a will.

"You have to give these babies something to eat," the nurse said, rearranging the blood pressure cuff on my arm.

I refrained from pointing out that the entire reason I'd skipped lunch was because I was stuck in my OB's office, at her request, and then here, in the hospital bed, being denied food, on the chance they decided to do a C-section in the next few hours. She handed me a small carton of orange juice and commanded me to drink it. The acid sloshed in my stomach and soured my mouth. My emergency pack of Tums was stashed in my backpack on a table halfway across the room. Where was Nona?

"Contractions?" the nurse said.

"Not really. I mean, I'm having one now..." I felt like I was being stuffed into a corset from the inside out. This wasn't anything new. I'd been having contractions for weeks, sometimes as many as six or eight an hour, but they never progressed to actual labor. When the doctor had checked my cervix, it hadn't even begun to soften. My body wasn't ready to give birth. Neither was I.

The nurse looked at the monitor, the numbers rising and climaxing and then falling. It looked like the diagram of Freytag's triangle I drew for my students, to explain the arc of a typical narrative. "You sure are. But nothing regular?"

"No," I exhaled.

"So Dr. Black said we'll keep you here for a couple hours?"

"I guess so."

"Okay, well, I'll be back to check on you in a little while. If you need anything, here's the call button."

I took a sip of juice and lay back. The nurse had turned down the volume on the baby's heart monitor but I watched the number and the graph. Steady, steady, steady, and then falling. The line dipped so far it looked like the side of a mountain. It wasn't supposed to be falling. I knew from the monitors in Dr. Black's office that if the baby moved enough she fell off the monitor entirely, but she still wasn't moving at all. I didn't know if I should panic.

"Hey, you okay?" Nona poked her head into the room.

"Yeah." I wanted to cry. "I'm sorry I scared you."

"You didn't scare me. But Lanita had an entire posse out looking for me. I was at lunch." She set her book bag and her coat down on the chair next to mine.

"I figured."

"Hey. I saw the Blonde in the hall, perky as ever."

"Oh joy." I shifted against the pillows. My hips hurt like hell. "Hey, can you ask the nurse if I can have something to eat? She made me drink this orange juice and if I don't eat something I'm going to puke."

"Sure. I'll be right back."

"This is all she would give me," she said, handing me a couple packs of saltines.

"That from the dad room?"

"They've got all kinds of things in there. Juice. Popsicles. Crackers."

The nurse came and went, checking my blood pressure, looking at the graph, then going to another room to check on a more legitimate patient, one actually laboring.

"I'm bored," I groaned. "Thank you for driving down here."

Her presence made it easier to pretend this was just another turn in an ongoing soap opera, not urgent medical intervention and imminent motherhood.

"Hey, I wouldn't let you be by yourself." She looked tired, like she'd been up half the night grading papers.

"You do have work."

"Eh, it's the first week, nothing's happening. You know how that goes."

"Any good gossip?"

"Oh the usual blow ups in meetings. I'll tell you about it later."

Everyone else I knew had gone back to work after the winter break. I wondered what life would be like for the next seven months, staying home with the baby until the fall semester started. Anything, I supposed, from long hours in front of the television snuggling to swaying with a screaming infant in my arms, dishes piling up in the sink. Or bundling her up in the car and going for drives, meeting friends at coffee shops and restaurants. Everyone I knew said that the reality of having a baby was nothing like the fantasy. What if I wasn't ready for the real thing? When I was a baby I cried, my mother said, for what seemed like six months nonstop. "I didn't know how to be a mother," she said, "and you didn't know how to be a baby." I'd wanted this child for so long but when it came down to it, I wondered if I would like being a mother. I was quick tempered and easily annoyed; the cat's 3:00 a.m. yowling put me over the edge in graduate school. Now, granted, a child wasn't a cat, but they were both completely dependent on me for food, water, shelter and security, and they took up about as much space, at least at first.

Dr. Black came in and started scrolling through the pages of the baby's heart graph. "How's she doing? Moving around anymore?"

"Not really," I said. "She's pretty obstinate."

She chuckled. "What's this?" she said to the nurse, marking the long deceleration.

"Oh, she was sitting up drinking some juice."

The doctor's eyes narrowed with disbelief. "I'm going to send you for a sono with the perinatologist," she said deliberately. "I'm not seeing anything really alarming here, but it's not what I'd like to see either. She'll be able to check blood flow in the umbilical cord. If the sono checks out, you can go home and we'll monitor you every other day until delivery. How does that sound?"

I nodded. I wasn't sure how scared I was supposed to be.

The nurse pushed me down the hall in the wheelchair while Nona trotted along by my side. A wheelchair seemed excessive, but I had to admit it was nice not having to lug an extra forty pounds around. It was only a slight exaggeration to say I couldn't walk anymore.

The baby was so big the sonogram only showed her piecemeal, part of the head, then crossed limbs, buttocks, spine. The doctor said she already weighed around six pounds.

"Wow," Nona said.

"Pretty cool, isn't it?" the perinatologist agreed, moving the transducer across my belly.

"How do you know the umbilical cord is okay?" Nona asked, echoing my doctor. She had her hand propped on her chin, like she was paying attention to a really interesting lecture. Welcome to Perinatology 101.

"We know it's okay because this baby looks great. She's moving. She's showing signs that she's practicing breathing. Her heart rate is fine. And she's growing."

She gave me a towel to rub the blue gel from my skin. I rubbed the top of my abdomen, where my daughter lay still.

"You should tell the pediatrician that one of the baby's kidneys is enlarged. It shouldn't be a big deal but one of those things that might be important to have in a medical history. I'll give Dr. Black a call and tell her you checked out fine."

"Thanks," I said.

"You know how to get back to L&D?" she asked Nona, as

I climbed back into the wheelchair.

We passed Dr. Black in the hall, wearing a hooded sweat-shirt instead of a winter coat. It was dinnertime; I'd been at her office since before lunch. I wondered what other patients she needed to check up on, how many babies she'd delivered that day. "I heard everything looks good. So go home. Do kick counts. And call the office in the morning to schedule an appointment for Friday. We'll do another NST and check your vitals. You'll come in again for your last appointment Monday morning. And unless something changes in the next few days, we're on for Monday night."

Terror rose up in me like the green sky before a tornado hit.

When we finally got home, I lay down on the couch with a can of Coke and let the corn syrup and caffeine rile the baby up. She kicked and punched, as if to say *here I am*, and I patted her bottom through my milk-pale skin. I sang to her, Sheryl Crow's "The First Cut is the Deepest," and eventually I fell asleep. She danced through the night like my uterus was the high school gym.

Other women get bachelorette parties. I got the Last Pre-Baby Weekend, courtesy of Cara and Blockbuster Video. I couldn't dance and couldn't drink, and the idea of taking a long ride in the truck to bounce the baby into labor, which Cara had concocted with a friend who had a ten-year-old, was out of the question.

I wanted her there.

I wanted her to go home.

I wanted her to know whatever I couldn't figure out that would make me comfortable.

I couldn't lie down. I couldn't sit up. And I most definitely couldn't stand.

Everyone was being kind. They called. They dropped by. Karen wanted to know if I'd bought a diaper pail yet. Cara and Alejandro loaded the dresser, the last piece of furniture for the nursery, into the back of their car and then assembled it. Nona showed up with long pieces of yellow and blue fabric to make quick curtains, and she sat sewing while Johnny Depp trotted around on the television in a pirate costume. She cooked pasta because the doula, who kept calling to check up on me, said I should carbo load, like I was doing a marathon. I wanted it over and I wasn't ready for it to be over. I resented the nine days or more that I wouldn't have my daughter in my body because my doctor didn't trust what it would do. I'd had one pregnancy cut far too short. I wanted every minute of this one.

I lay in bed, breathing softly and counting the number of times the baby kicked. Some of the books said she should move six times in an hour and others ten, and they all said hiccoughs didn't count. Even on the verge of delivery, I had no idea what a fetal hiccough felt like, though she must have done them all the time. All I knew was the baby was still slower than she used to be, and my blood pressure was rising, it seemed, by the minute. I hated that the doctor was right. I had no business being pregnant after thirty-eight weeks.

I couldn't sleep. I tried to clean. I tried to get my desk in order and all the laundry done. I still hadn't packed my bag.

(Birth)

WE DRIVE THROUGH THE NIGHT. Lit only by reflectors marking the center of the lane, the highway feels dangerous and unfamiliar. This last trip to the hospital is somehow both long and impossibly short, the fifth time in a week that I've traveled back and forth, alone, or with Cara, or with Nona, who is now filling me in on the gossip at work and asking me to invent a story for her nephew, only I can't think of anything except what is going to happen to me when this car stops. Since the day I met Dr. Black, this is the moment that has filled me with dread, the IV in my arm and the stir-rupped bed, and the monitor with its printout, charting the geography of pain.

I have read enough to know I do not want to give birth in a hospital. I have read enough to know I want to be in a hospital with a neonatal intensive care unit if something goes wrong. The disconnect between these ideas leaves me panicked. I rub circles on my abdomen, big as it will ever be, and tell my daughter it will be okay.

"Did you bring something to eat?" I ask Nona, because I know the day will be long. It is 9:00 at night; the baby will not be born until sometime tomorrow, or even the next day. When Dr. Black started talking about Pitocin, a drug that stimulates uterine contractions and known to make labor unbearable, I referenced an article my doula had given me on "gentle induction," hoping to use the drug to help labor along rather than force my body into doing something it clearly isn't ready to do. My doctor said, smiling in that southern belle way of hers, "now we don't want you to be in labor for days, do we?" And clearly, I don't want to be in labor for days but I do want my body to do what it needs to do to give birth to my daughter, and if that means forty-eight hours of labor, well, that's what I will do. But she smiled and in the end I signed the papers that said I understood the risks of the drug because she'd scared me into believing that was my only real choice. *Clotting disorder,* she said. *Placental insufficiency,* she said. *Stillbirth,* she said, smiling her best Texas smile.

"I'm going to stop at the convenience store by the hospital, get crackers and juice or something," Nona says, pulling into the gas station down the street from the hospital. I wait in the parking lot while she runs inside, and I think about asking her to turn the car around, take me home, wait the days that my body wants to take before labor starts on its own. At my exam that morning, my cervix had not yet begun to open. The process feels doomed before it even begins. The words *"high risk"* hang heavy around my neck and I try to tell myself that I need to be there, strapped to the monitors, making sure this sleepy, refusing-to-move baby and I would both be born.

When we arrive at the hospital we carry our bags and extra pillows across the parking lot and through the lobby and the long hallway to the elevator. We walk past the perinatologist's office we'd visited only days ago, and I check myself in at the nurse's desk. It feels like a police station, or the principal's office at the high school, with its high counters and computer monitors, boxes of Kleenex and hand-sanitizer.

After I am taken to my room, after I put on the blue and white hospital gown, Nona takes a picture of me standing there, hand on my abdomen, before I climb into bed. I haven't slept than more than a few hours in what must be days. The nurses come and go, changing shifts, asking me questions, taking my blood pressure, watching the baby's heart rate on the monitor. They are busy tonight, a Monday night, delivering babies of women who were induced that morning. Eventually they remember me, strapped to the monitor, and they put a pill, Cytotec, up next to my cervix to allow it to ripen.

Sometime as today becomes tomorrow, the contractions begin in earnest. I will my body to open. The doctor told me that if labor progresses sufficiently on its own, I won't need Pitocin. I want give birth on my own terms. Each time my uterus tightens I feel like I am a lone traveler to a familiar country. Nona sleeps on the chair that folds down like a twin bed. Over and over, I read the row of plastic bracelets on my arm, all with my name, my doctor's name, my blood type and the reason for admission, pre-induction of labor. They are passport and visa for this long journey. I think about the book I brought with me, resting in my finally-packed bag with some T-shirts and onesies and little white socks for the baby and a pair of clean pajamas and toiletries for me. It is a perverse vacation, the hospital room with an armoire like you'd find in a fancy hotel, and all the surgical supplies hidden from view. I think of Margaret Atwood's novel *The Handmaid's Tale*. I think I can hear someone screaming in the next room.

I try not to wake Nona. I moan a sleepy moan every two or three minutes until finally she rouses herself and we are in a space outside of time, full of nothing but breathing and pain. Then the sun rises and doula shows up and my doctor shows up and a new nurse shows up and I am nothing but a body coiled around itself. My doctor had said a nurse would rouse me to shower and prepare for the day. None of this has gone according to plan.

"I'm going to try to break your water. Open your legs," Dr. Black says, "like a frog," and I want to laugh, but her hand is inside me when the contraction hits and all I can do is grab Nona's hand and cry. She puts inserts a stick, a probe, a spoon, and I am there fourteen months ago with Dr. C in the operating room scooping out my son like an avocado.

"She keeps moving back," the doctor says, and I do not know if she means the baby or me, both of us receding from her touch. She has the nurse press on the top of my uterus while she tries again.

When the amniotic sac breaks, it is like an ocean crashing; liquid pools beneath me. "It's warm," is the only thing I can think to say.

"Yes, it's the temperature of your body."

Oh, oh, oh.

All day I move from the bed to the rocking chair to the big rubber birth ball, trying to find a comfortable position, letting gravity work on me. All day the nurse comes in and looks at the monitor and puts her hand between my legs and take notes. Every time the doctor comes in, she pushes buttons on my IV pole, upping the level of medication. When the contractions come, I feel like I am going to split in two. The books all say there is a slow rise and then a peak and a fall, just like a good story, but there is no exposition here, no build up, no dramatic pause, just one climax after another, every two minutes all day. It's like being in a vise.

Even Debbie, the birth doula I have hired to help see me through this process naturally, tells me to take the medication they keep offering, that it might allow me to rest. My body is a tuning fork. The vibrations never end. Stress rolls off me in waves.

"The baby's fine," she says. "The baby's fine." She's been watching the graph. She has six children of her own, used to be a nurse.

Eventually I concede, take half a pill the nurse hands me, probably that margarita drug. All it does it make me woozy, and I close my eyes and watch the red spikes flicker against the inside of my eyelids. The pain in my uterus is still sharp, unfathomable. Debbie and Nona take turns rubbing my back. I clutch a heating pad full of rice against my abdomen. I press it so hard against my belly that even the monitor loses track of the pain.

I only know time from the doctor's announcement of her comings and goings. By 3:00 I have only dilated a pathetic few centimeters. My doctor increases the medication and leaves.

At 5:00 she puts a probe up inside my uterus, alongside the baby's head, to chart the contractions more adequately. My body isn't working hard enough, she says. She ups the medication and leaves.

I steal small sips of water from a plastic cup and cry, I can't do this anymore. I can't I can't I can't.

"The doctor will be here in half an hour. You can wait that long, can you wait that long?" I hold on to Nona's voice like the oars of a boat, rowing me down a barely navigable stream. We keep crashing into rocks along the shore.

It's 7:00 when the doctor comes and she looks at me and says in an I-told-you-so voice, "Are you ready for an epidural now?"

I look at Nona and I look at Debbie and I am crying when I nod and Dr. Black says, gently now, "Either that will help move things along or we will have to do a C-section."

I lean against Debbie and hold Nona's hands while the anesthesiologist puts a needle in my back—again, I told myself I would never do this, again— but then I feel nothing, absolutely nothing, from the chest down, not even the baby wiggling, and I finally close my eyes and rest.

The doctor comes in at nine—it's been twenty-four hours since I was admitted—and still there is no change. "We just have to get you delivered," she says. Cephalopelvic disproportion. A failure of labor to progress. They wheel the bed down the hall. In only twenty minutes I am prepped for surgery, all of us wearing blue shower caps. The baby's heart rate is still good on the monitor—Nona keeps checking—and they tape electrodes to my chest.

It is cold and I am shivering and before I even know the doctor has made an incision, the baby's cry fills the room, mad as hell.

I hear myself ask in a popsicle-colored voice, "What does she look like?" and someone, Nona I suppose, says, "She's beautiful!"

My memory of that night is covered in shadow, more than I'd like to admit. After they tugged the baby from my body, after they cleaned and swaddled her, after they put her face next to mine so we were cheek to cheek, Nona followed her to wherever they took newly newborn babies to have them weighed and measured and cleaned, while the doctor sewed and stapled and taped me back together.

The times stamped on the digital photos reveal I was alone— not alone, I'm sure a nurse was with me—without Nona or the baby for several hours. I do not remember sleeping. I do not remember anything but the coldness of the room (I was wrapped in a stack of white blankets), and the pulse ox monitor on my finger and the heart monitor taped up on top of my breasts. They showed up, all of them, Nona and the baby and Debbie with the camera, and it was close to midnight, February 11, a night I once associated with the death of Sylvia Plath. A night I once wrote melodramatic poems and scratched a razor blade along the pale skin of my ankle. It was, really, the first day of my daughter's life, the day my whole world changed.

They say that mothers always touch their newborns in a particular order, something innate as giving birth itself. I took her hand in mine, I touched her ruddy cheek, I looked into her slate gray eyes and I wondered if, eventually, they would be green or brown. I would like to think it was my idea to put her to my breast, but I'm sure it was the nurse who showed me how to hold her, who arranged the gowns and blankets so my child could drink. I held her, and I whispered her name and cried.

It was all so surreal.

I still couldn't feel my legs or really sit up and I'm sure that was a blessing. They would keep me on the epidural until sometime the next day, leaving me immobile, tacked to the bed like a bug on a nail. They took the baby to the nursery and wheeled me to my room—Nona was already asleep there on the other bed—and though I literally hadn't slept in days, I couldn't. I wanted the baby back, they told me I could have her with me, and the hours ticked by on the clock and we were separate. I missed her weight, pressed against my ribcage, where she'd been for months. I hadn't fully processed the fact that giving birth was the end of being pregnant, a state I'd very much enjoyed.

Nona told me later I got a bit crazy. I wonder if she thinks that now, after she has also given birth and had abdominal surgery in the same day.

The nurse finally brought the baby to me in the morning, after the pediatrician had a chance to look her over. She was cold, the nurse said; I needed to keep her in a blanket held to my chest or she needed to go back to the nursery under a warmer. I held her against me, in her pink and blue striped cap, with yellow mittens on her hands, and she curled into a ball the exact size and shape of my abdomen before her birth. I kept reading the information on the pink card taped to the plastic hospital bassinet. 6 lb 12 oz, 19.5 inches. February 10, 2004, 9:32 p.m. Somehow the words made her real.

In the women's wing of the hospital, I wasn't any different than any other new mother, though Nona said the staff referred to me as *the one who tried to go natural*, which I supposed was better than *the one who used a sperm donor*. When the nurse had checked me in on the night of the induction, she'd asked me if the baby's father would be in the delivery room.

"He's a sperm donor," I said. I rolled the words around in my mouth, feeling their shape, wondering how often that question would come up in daily life as a parent.

"Yes," she chuckled, "aren't they all? I just need to know if he'll be allowed to see the baby."

"No. He's a sperm donor," I repeated, enunciating each syllable. I looked at Nona for reassurance that I hadn't lost the ability to speak English.

"Oh, you mean, really?"

"Yeah, really."

Now I was just another woman who'd given birth, entitled to a free black diaper bag full of Pampers and formula samples like anyone else. More than two years later, I still keep it in the car with spare clothes. It came with an ice pack to chill breastmilk, with the name of the formula company stamped on it, and I found that mildly amusing. Maybe someday I could tell that story to my gender studies students, when we talked about consumer culture.

Tucked inside were fliers were about "mommy and me" classes and breastfeeding support hot lines, infant safety precautions and daily logs to record intake and output, which apparently was the most important thing to do when you are a new mother. Every time a nurse came in, she asked to see the log, which recorded minutes I nursed her on each side and how many diapers I changed. There was also a pretend birth certificate, with the baby's footprints stamped on it, and they looked ridiculously elongated compared to the feet I cradled in my hands. (I vaguely wondered if they'd given me the wrong baby, but when I looked at her profile it was exactly the same as what it seen in those sonogram photos over the months.) And the paperwork for the real birth certificate and social security number, which I needed to fill out before being discharged. The baby, it seemed, needed a name. And soon enough she would owe taxes.

I didn't want to talk to anybody. I called people, left weepy messages on answering machines, like *hey, I'm a mom now*, but I didn't really want to talk. I let Nona and Cara answer the phone and deal with the people in the nursery and whatever was going on back home. I wanted to be alone with my child and let the world go on without me. I could stare at the baby all day, like a television show that never went off the air and never got boring. Flowers piled up in the room, daisies and roses and who knows what else, in purple plastic vases and green ceramic vases and spray-painted baskets. There were half-drunk bottles of water and containers of juice from the Dad room, and the books I'd brought with me—somehow convinced I might actually do work while the baby slept—piled on a Formica countertop.

When it came down to it, the hospital was boring, and I felt like I was in the Panopticon, always under surveillance. The baby had a nurse and I had a nurse, and one or the other was always coming in with a thermometer or a shot of heparin or a cup of pills. Both of us had regularly scheduled blood tests and physical exams. In the morning we saw my doctor and the pediatrician, and in the afternoons the lactation consultants would come by, press the tops of my breasts, and praise me on my technique. Apparently I had good breasts, at least when it came to feeding. I thought about calling Dr. Boy to tell him.

When my mother arrived on Thursday we took slow walks down the corridors, me pushing the plastic bassinet like a walker. When we walked too far, past the double doors by the NICU, an alarm sounded from the security gizmo strapped to the baby's leg like an oversized anklet. I felt like I was kidnapping my own baby, like an antique doll kept on display at a museum.

They finally let us go home on Saturday, in the middle of a freak Texas snowstorm, so long as I agreed to bring the baby back to have her bilirubin count and weight checked on Monday. "It's really coming down out there," Dr. Banks said when she discharged us, "I'm trying to get everyone checked out before it freezes." A nurse unhooked the security monitor from the baby's ankle so I could dress her for the long ride home.

It's snowing outside. I can see the snow blowing across the sidewalk from the rocker, where I sit holding the baby, watching her suck a dream nipple in her sleep. She wears a blanket sleeper patterned with yellow ducks, a matching white and yellow cap on her head. Before we left the hospital, Nona helped me dress her in layers of footed sleepers; the snowsuit I'd bought on sale—a fleecy white thing with the brown ears of a bear—looked about three sizes too big. My mother took a picture on the digital camera, the two of us hunched over the baby, our hands forever fastening zippers and snaps. In it, Nona looks proud and worn out as any new parent, her brown hair falling in tired strands around her face, while my blue maternity shirt billows around my abdomen in the shape of loss. I wonder how this child will change us.

Outside, it is colder than I knew Texas could get; the room warms with our syncopated breaths and the slow glide of the rocker. I send Mom outside to snap a photo for the baby's album; it is Valentine's Day and her very first snowstorm rolled into one. It is, I think, a storybook ending after all. We are surrounded by gifts, by boxes of books and clothes, by balloons and streamers and vases stuffed with flowers. Sometime in the past week, Cara and Nona managed to hang a plush purple moon and yellow star over the crib, and assemble a mobile with animal shapes. This is the room of a child who is wanted and adored, welcomed by a makeshift family of friends. More than three years ago, I made the decision to become a single mother; today I am far from alone.

In the refrigerator is a bowl of Cara's *arroz con pollo* and another of Alejandro's Turkish green beans in tomato sauce, two of my favorite dishes. My mother goes out to the store for the handful of things we need—a mirror to see the baby while I drive, some extra lap pads and diaper cream, orange juice with calcium, Hershey's kisses in pink wrappers. For the first time, I am alone with my daughter in our home, the cat curled like a cliché at my slippered feet. The baby nurses greedily, our newly severed bodies skin to skin. There is no other way to say this: she smells like everything good in the world, a mix of Pampers and Johnson's shampoo, and the deep ocean of my womb.

Once I spent too many lonely hours dreaming up scenes like this. Once I never thought this moment to be possible. I look at the bookcase—the one Nona and I painted together, an old piece of fake wood made new with yellow and blue paint, with stenciled letter blocks on the side. Someday my daughter will put her favorite stories on these shelves, *Mother Goose* and *Goodnight Moon, Nancy Drew* and *Little House on the Prairie*. Someday she will take a paint brush and cover all this up, make the shelves purple or orange, with big obnoxious flowers or polka dots and stripes, and I will tell her about what it felt like to be pregnant and decorating this for her, writing the name of a child who wasn't yet born. One day I will tell her the story of how she came to be, a story of long walks on the track and longer drives down a Texas highway, a story of glass vials and hypodermic needles, sonograms and garden gnomes, a story not of a man and a woman but a love story nonetheless. Tomorrow I will send a birth announcement to Dr. C, something I have been waiting these long months to do. Perhaps she will print the photo and hang it on the corkboard outside the nurse's lounge at the clinic, for this child is part of her story, too. But here, now, we are mother and child, Robin Paula and Hannah Sadie. Her birth certificate has been sent to the state of Texas, and we are home.

Afterword/Afterbirth

THERE ARE MANY STORIES I could tell about Hannah's first year. I could tell you about the first time I took her out alone, a five-minute car ride to the pediatrician for her two-week checkup, how I nearly dropped her carrier in the waiting room when my abdomen burned and my sutures pulled, and the wonderful nurse (whose name was Daryl or Dwight) offered to carry her for me. Or I could tell you about the nights I drove the long circle around town while Hannah cried in the backseat (I was never so grateful for the drive-thru lane at the Starbucks that finally opened just off the highway in town) but inevitably, as soon as I lugged her car seat back inside, she'd wake up wailing. I took a lot of long showers her first few months, as the sound she really liked was running water, and the steam helped unplug her nose. Or I could tell you about my first day back at work when she was six months, after I melted her bottles on the stove while checking my email, which should have taught me some kind of cosmic lesson about the dangers of multitasking. But I'll save those for another book. This one ends the only place it can.

Dr. Boy rode Hannah on his shoulders through the aisles of Whole Foods, her spit-covered hands tapping the top of his head like a bongo drum. I raced up and down, scavenging for applesauce and jars of mashed bananas and winter squash, filling our cart. We were just like any other couple on a lunchtime rendezvous, a baby passed between us in a wordless exchange, except we weren't really a couple at all. I thought how good he looked holding her, her small body an extension of his.

"You don't need to carry her," I said. "We do have a stroller."

"Not a problem. Just letting her see a little more of the world. It's really different up here you know."

"Funny." Something akin to longing broke open in my chest like a starburst. I wasn't sure what I was doing. We hadn't seen him in more than a year, since Hannah was about three months old and he finally made the drive up to check out my offspring. He'd watched me nurse her with a puzzled look, like his boat had just landed on a desert island and he'd stumbled upon the only natives. I thought, just maybe the long thread of desire that held us together like a phone line had been severed for good. But after I'd scheduled Hannah's appointment with the allergist, which was only a few blocks from his place in the city, I'd suggested we meet for lunch. I needed to say goodbye.

When Nona and I had walked across campus in September talking about the job list that had just come out and fantasizing about where we could be living next year, I hadn't really imagined anything would come of it. Still, she came over one weekend and bounced Hannah on her lap while I sat at the computer and tried to write a passable cover letter and writing sample, certain that that going on the market, as we referred to it, was an exercise in futility. I could have counted the number of applications I sent on my small girl's toes. They were all within four hours driving distance of Chicago. The proverbial stars aligned. The week of Hannah's first birthday I left her with Cara and Alejandro, who said they could use the practice parenting for a weekend, so I could attend a campus interview. Now we were moving to Michigan, back to winters that lasted from October to May. Now I needed to say my goodbyes.

When I finished gathering supplies for our long car drive north, we sat outside eating, Hannah with applesauce all over her face. "Bye bye," she said to the cars, pulling out of the parking lot. Dr. Boy snapped pictures on his camera like a doting father. People came and went, carts filled with fresh salads and organic cantaloupes, chlorine-free diapers and baby wipes. One woman had a cart filled with nothing but carrots and sweet potatoes. I remembered the woman I'd seen feeding her baby sweet potato, spooning it straight from the crisp baked skin to her child's open mouth, my first fantasy of motherhood.

I wanted to cry.

"I guess I won't see you again before you go," he said. The tone of his voice was unreadable.

"Probably not."

"It will be strange, not having you here." He snapped another picture of Hannah on the digital camera.

"It will be strange living in a place without you. I mean, even though I didn't see you very often, you were always just an hour away." I don't know if he knew it, but even in those months after the miscarriage when I wouldn't talk to him, he'd been my Texas safety net.

I shook Hannah's bottle and popped off the cap. She drank it greedily. "Baa," she sighed, the nipple hanging out of her mouth.

"We're going to have to get going soon," I said, smoothing her hair. "So she sleeps in the car," I offered by way of explanation. I knew I couldn't go back to his place, that if I did, I might never want to leave.

He bounced Hannah in his arms while I loaded her stroller and our groceries into the car. The trunk was full of jarred baby food and some fruit for me. And on top was a fruit tart I would savor later, remembering how light I felt that summer I was pregnant and the whole world smelled like lemon filling.

"All set," I said, taking Hannah from him and settling her into her car seat with the rest of her bottle and a pacifier.

In the parking lot, Dr. Boy cradled me against him, his hand around my neck.

"You be good to your mommy, Hannah Sadie," he said, poking his head into the backseat. "Let her sleep every once in a while."

"Stay in touch, you," I said. "I don't even think I have your address."

"Wherever I am, I have this." He held up his cell phone.

"I haven't managed to get into that habit yet." I pushed my hair behind my ears. "I'll give you my new number when I get it. You know, so you can harass me at all hours of the night."

"Any time."

"You going home?"

"Nah. I think I'll sit here for a while and write." He patted the computer bag at his hip. "You know, so I can make my big break and go to New York."

"We'll talk," I said.

"Yeah, we'll talk." I gave him a hug to last and got into the car. Hannah squawked in the backseat.

I weaved through side streets until I found myself on the highway, headed north. Mile by mile, I said goodbye. Goodbye Dr. Boy, goodbye Dr. C, goodbye goodbye goodbye.

The car was packed tight with everything that mattered, the trunk layered with pillows and duffel bags, Hannah's umbrella stroller, and the last box of books from my office, student grades and works-in-progress resting on top. In the backseat, Hannah was strapped into her Britax carseat, facing everything the movers hadn't taken with them. She kicked furiously against the upholstered seat and flung her pacifiers, which flew like silicone butterflies let loose in the sun. One whacked me on the head. My mom sat next to her, with a bag of books and baby toys at her feet. Pistachio was next to me in the passenger seat, scared into silence, her dog-sized pink carrier resting on top of her now empty litter box, wrapped in doubled garbage bags. I found Dar Williams in the CD case, and thought of how empty I felt when I first listened to her work, that long last year of graduate school with my grandmother dying, when all I wanted was a child.

Cara and Alejandro stood at the edge of their driveway, Alejandro holding little Eli and waving his chubby arms like his favorite soccer player had just scored the winning goal. I thought about how hard I had fought to have Hannah and how hard Eli fought to make his way into the world and all the trips to the park that our children wouldn't be able to take, not together at least. I wondered how much of all this, if anything, Hannah would remember, the long winding road we lived on and the huge white cross next to the apartment, the rows of mailboxes and the laundry room smelling of Tide. A grasshopper landed on the windshield, a tiny green stowaway.

How I would miss them.

My girl jabbered in the backseat, "ba ba ba ba ba," clenching her fists like she was milking a cow, universal baby signing for milk. I turned the key in the ignition and we were off, going North this time instead of South, past the fruit stands and antique shops, past the lake and the Oklahoma border. We drove into the sunset. The highway stretched ahead of us like the crisp pages of a new book.

Author's Note

This is a work of nonfiction. In all significant (and most insignificant) factual and emotional ways, the story told in these pages is true. However, for the sake of narrative coherence, the timeline has been gently compressed, and most of the real people featured here have been given pseudonyms in the interests of preserving their privacy. This is my story.

Acknowledgements

A big pot of chili and eternal gratitude to the women who nourished me in Texas: Bernice, Bonnie, Carol, Elena, Ellen, Gayle, Hanna, Kylie. And to Beth, Lindy, and Nick, who gave me focus and energy when I needed it most.

And in Michigan: Alissa, Melissa, Kristina, Zarena, who saw me through the second half of the journey. The highway always brings me back to you.

Thanks also to Lee Martin and Judith Roof, who provided feedback on early drafts.

To my mother who taught me everything I know about being a single mom.

And, Walton, without you there would be no story. Thank you.

Robin Silbergleid is the author of two chapbooks of poetry *Pas de Deux: Prose and Other Poems* (2006) and *Frida Kahlo, My Sister* (2014). Born and raised in the Midwest, she holds both an M.F.A. and Ph.D. from Indiana University. She lives in East Lansing, Michigan, where she directs the Creative Writing Program at Michigan State University and raises her two children.